Familiar Spirits The Unseen Enemies

John Deby Edukugho

Copyright © 2004 by John Deby Edukugho

Familiar Spirits The Unseen Enemies
by John Deby Edukugho

Printed in the United States of America

ISBN 1-594671-28-1

All rights reserved. No part of this publication may be reproduced or transmitted in any form or by any means without written permission of the author.

Unless otherwise indicated, Bible quotations are taken from the King James Version. Copyright © 1988 by B. B. Kirkbride Bible Company, Inc., Indianapolis, Indiana.

Xulon Press
www.XulonPress.com

Xulon Press books are available in bookstores everywhere, and on the Web at www.XulonPress.com.

DEDICATION

First of all, I want to dedicate this book to the Almighty God, then, to all the Saints of God who are in the business of winning souls for Jesus Christ.

Also, to my precious wife Kate Kodekode who has been a very good help especially when I had the dire need to sum up courage. To my mother Elizabeth Amurunoghotse who was always reminding me of God's calling upon my life, when like Prophet Jonah, I tried to run away giving my first love to business and politics.

ACKNOWLEDGEMENT

I would earnestly like to acknowledge here the Holy Spirit, who over the years has brought to my awareness strategic warfare against evil powers of darkness; to expose and dismantle their wicked manifestations in human lives in the name of Jesus Christ.

I would also like to thank the following brethren for their immense contribution: SENI ADELAGUN, TUNDE OGUNDIPE AND KEHINDE AWE, who painstakingly went through the scripts with helpful suggestions.

CONTENTS

Acknowledgement vii

Chapter One
    The Unseen Enemies..11

Chapter Two
    The Manifestations of Familiar Spirits in
    Human Life 25

Chapter Three
    Familiar Spirits and Their Modes of Attack...............43

Chapter Four
    Familiar Spirit and Mediums.......................................67

Chapter Five
    Curses and Covenants 77

Chapter Six
    Believer's Authority 107

Chapter Seven
    Binding and Loosing...115

Chapter Eight
    Believers Victory Over Satan 127

CHAPTER ONE

THE UNSEEN ENEMIES

A spirit is an unseen intelligent being. Some spirits can inhabit both human and animal bodies.

1 Corinthians 2: 11-12: clearly differentiates three kinds of spirit:

a. The Spirit of God (Holy Spirit)
b. The spirit of man (Human spirit)
c. The spirit of the World (Satanic spirit)

There are also good spirits like angels that exist in the Kingdom of God and evil spirits (demons) that operate under the captaincy of satan. The good spirits outnumber the evil spirits. For the primary purpose of spiritual warfare, this book will concentrate on FAMILIAR SPIRITS.

A familiar spirit is an evil spirit, which operates to serve satan's purpose in the lives of individual persons or family units. It is an evil spirit that is very familiar with a person, family, ancestral lineage, a place or a thing. It often manifests as an influencing or controlling spirit; a servient or guiding spirit to its medium or conjurer. The word familiar spirit appears sixteen times in the Bible.

The phrase "Familiar Spirits" is the Hebrew word OB (pronounced "ahv", a parallel term in Greek is known as EGGASRIMUTHOS, which means "Ventriloquist". A ventriloquist demon produces in the medium (human vessel) in whom he dwells, strange noises of high sounds and mutters low sounds. The demon could project sounds out of the ground, bring it up from the table or from the ceiling.

Frequently, he controls the vocal cords of the medium or conjurer in a clever impersonation of the living and the dead. This type of activity is described in **Isaiah 29:4**

"And thou shalt be brought down, and shall speak out of the ground and thy speech shall be low out of the dust, and thy voice shall be, as one that hath a familiar spirit, out of the ground, and thy speech shall whisper out of the dust"

The term "Familiar" is used mostly in the Old Testament to describe the alleged spirit of a deceased person. This spirit was on intimate terms with the deceased, very familiar with him when he was alive. Another parallel term in Hebrew is (Yada) pronounced (Yaw-dah) which means a knowing one; an unseen acquaintance; a knowing spirit.

A familiar spirit is a KNOWING SPIRIT possessing accurate knowledge about people and capable of communicating this knowledge to those whom they serve. They are very deceptive demons; spying spirits doing reconnaissance job for the devil. They are lawless spirits who monitor individual human being on this planet earth.

One of the most descriptive accounts of this is found in **1 Samuel Chapter 28:** when king Saul visited the witch of Endor to seek her assistance to contact the spirit of the dead prophet Samuel. The witch of Endor, as a medium, called up her guiding spirit. Surprisingly, the conjured spirit appeared impersonating the dead prophet Samuel, this spirit was the familiar spirit operating against prophet Samuel when he was alive and at his death was still hanging around, and is able to impersonate all the characteristics of prophet Samuel.

Consulting the spirits of the dead is an old time satanic tradition that is still being practiced up till now. These practitioners are called necromancers. Nevertheless, this does not disprove genuine prophets of God who by the leading of the Holy Spirit communicate things to people by word of knowledge or word of wisdom or by direct visions and dreams they received from God.

However, one should not be deceived by false prophets, diviners, witches, wizards, fortune tellers, necromancers and other mediums because in the spirit world your life is like a history book, so do not be surprised if someone reads a chapter or two in your life history book through occultic means and tells you things which they have no natural way of knowing, like foretelling your future or recalling past occurrences.

The truth is that by the aid of familiar or servient spirits many ungodly persons can peep into the spirit realm to spy a few events in your life history book and reveal such to you.

The Bible warns us of such fake prophets or seers and instructs us in **_Matthew 7: 15-20_** to judge them by their fruits. Examine the fruits in the lives of the people who are predicting or prophesying to you even if their predictions and prophecies come to pass.

The Bible confirms that there are books in the spirit realm that cannot be reached by natural means. **_Revelation 20:12_** explains:

> *"I saw the dead, small and great, stand before God, and the books were opened;*

and another book was opened, which is the book of life; and the dead were judged out of those things which were written in the books, according to their works".

These mediums can only peep into the books under the permissive will of God. If their fruit is rotten then you will not have any problem in determining their source of information and power. Remember that satan still retains the power and wisdom that God gave to him, though he has corrupted them to do evil; so he often appears as an angel of light and truth in his manifestations, which he is not.

BE CAREFUL! BE WARNED!

It is evident from biblical standpoint that no person whether a spiritualist, necromancer, herbalist, native doctor, sorcerer and even a prophet of God can speak to an actual dead person. It is a common practice for these spiritual liars to deceive people that they communicate with the dead, especially the so-called "SPIRITS OF OUR ANCESTORS OR THE DEAD ".

In the African custom and that of other nationalities these tricksters actually speak to and get their information from spirits who know intimately or are familiar with a dead person when he was alive or his family history.

"The dust (body) will return to the earth as it was, and the spirit will return to God who gave it".
Ecclesiastes 3:20

The account of Lazarus and the rich man in **LUKE 16:19-31** will throw more light. Lazarus died and went to Abraham's bosom and then the rich man died and went to hell. When a person dies his soul is either going to paradise or to hell. At last the rich man could not cross over to Lazarus, and Lazarus could not return to earth to warn the rich man's brothers about the torments and horrors of hell. He could not speak to them any way. There is no connection between the spirit of the dead and a living person.

It is also unscriptural to ask for a dead saint to intercede in prayers for a living saint. Praying through a dead saint of God is a function of commonsense, it is not a biblical injunction. Jesus instructed us to pray through Him to the Father. The Holy Spirit and the LIVING SAINTS also help to intercede on our behalf. **<u>Romans 8:26</u>**

> *"Likewise the spirit also helpeth our infirmities: for we know not what we should pray as we ought: <u>but the spirit himself maketh intercession for us with groanings which cannot be uttered</u>"*

It is obvious from biblical accounts that no being has power to do anything with your spirit when you are dead except God, your creator.

The Bible also gives us an insight of the happenings in the spirit world. It proved that when your body dies and goes to the grave, your spirit, the real you goes to be with God, if you believe in Jesus Christ as your saviour or to be with the devil in hell if you reject Jesus Christ by God's own divine decree.

TYPES AND FORMS

The spirits that have become familiar with one person may not be necessarily familiar with another person. The spirits that are familiar with a person, place, family or thing are precisely their familiar spirits.

Your familiar spirits are those evil spirits that have been lurking around you for a very longtime. They know you intimately and you may not know them, neither can you see them with your eyes because they are spirits. They can only be discerned by the help of the Holy Spirit. They are also known as trailing spirits.

Familiar spirits are very close unseen intelligent beings operating for satan in order to influence the thoughts and activities of human beings and record information about their lives in their satanic books, computers, audio tapes, video tapes and discs; which are subsequently kept in archives and libraries in the satanic kingdom. The records are made against various families passing from one generation to another. These spirits could also be identified with certain tribes, communities or race. They are responsible for certain family, tribal, communal and racial evil traits. They influence both cultural and societal values.

> *Your familiar spirits are those evil spirits that have been lurking around you for a very longtime. They know you intimately and you may not know them, neither can you see them with your eyes because they are spirits.*

They have various kinds of names by which they could be discerned and their classification is exclusively related to their mode of activities or area of assignment. There are thousands of million of them operating universally, doing their master Satan's bidding.

The commonly discerned ones manifest as the spirits of lying, lust, envy, stealing, madness, vengeance, greed, infirmity, fear, anxiety, anger, strife, deceit, doubt, destruction, setback, rejection. Others are idolatry, alcoholism, deaf and dumb, wretchedness, witchcraft, hatred, emulations, accidents, poverty, rebellion, violence, death, pride, stagnancy, incest, failure, disappointment, inheritance, marital destruction, mental illness, unsuccessfulness etc. The list is inexhaustible because their operations and assignments are multidimensional. They may operate individually or in group under a group head.

Have you heard people regrettably complaining about certain reoccurring evil influences or experiences in their lives? They often complain of being liars, drunkards, sexually promiscuous, quick tempered, easily prompted to violence, highly critical of others even when they are doing well, embarrassingly dishonest.

They have that irresistible urge to steal, kill, commit suicide, be rebellious against their parents or superiors; they have survived repeated motor accidents, nothing they lay their hands on ever prospers, they have been experiencing unabated cycles of disappointment, hurtings, failures, poverty, insufficiency and misfortunes. These worrisome experiences are inexhaustible. Such person, especially believers, needs counseling and if necessary deliverance ministry.

Familiar spirits are very deceitful, destructive and are often behind these evil occurrences, except they are discerned by the power of the Holy Spirit and cast out from their victims' lives by the authority of Jesus Christ, they will maintain their destructive influences until the person's death. Their operation will terminate only at their victims' funeral if they are not bound and cast out.

Let us consider a biblical example of how a familiar spirit operates as contained in:-

Genesis 12: 10-17

> *"And there was a famine in the land; and Abram went down to Egypt to sojourn there; for the famine was grievous in the land, and it came to pass, when he was*

come near to enter into Egypt, that he said unto Sar-a-i his wife, behold now, I know that thou art a fair woman to look upon: Therefore it shall come to pass, when the Egyptians shall see thee, that they shall say, this is his wife: and they will kill me, but they will save thee alive. <u>Say I pray thee, thou art my sister, that it may be well with me for thy sake; and my soul shall live because of thee.</u> And it came to pass, that, when Abram was come into Egypt, the Egyptians beheld the woman that she was very fair, the princes also of Pharaoh saw her, commended her before Pharaoh; and the woman was taken into pharaoh's house, and he entreated Abram well for her sake; and he had sheep, and oxen, and asses and menservants, and maidservant, and she asses, and camels, and the lord plagued Pharaoh and his house with great plagues because of Sar-a-i Abram's wife.

Abram, the friend of God, the man who believed God so much, influenced by the spirit of FEAR called his wife his sister. He lied! Now let's see Abraham again being messed up by a familiar spirit called the LYING SPIRIT in:-

Genesis 20: 1-5

"And Abraham journeyed from thence toward the south country, and dwelled between Kadesh and Shur, and sojourned in Gerar.

<u>And Abraham said of Sarai his wife, She is my sister; and Abimelech King of Gerar</u>

<u>sent, and took Sarah.</u> *But God came to Abimelech in a dream by night, and said to him, behold, thou art but a dead man, for the woman, which thou hast taken, for she is a man's wife. But Abimelech had not come near her: and he said, Lord, wilt thou slay also a righteous nation? <u>Said he not unto me, She is my sister?</u>*

And she, even she herself, he is my brother in the integrity of my heart and innocence of my hands have I done this".

Look at this new scenario.

ABRAHAM LIED! SARAH LIED!

Satan is aware of the great covenant God has made with Abram in *<u>Genesis 17:7, 15-16</u>*

"<u>And I will establish my covenant between me and thee and thy seed after thee in their generations for an everlasting covenant, to be a God unto thee, and to thy seed after thee. (vs. 7)</u>

God said unto Abraham, As for Sarai thy wife, thou shall not call her name Sarai, but Sarah shall her name be.
And I will bless her, and give thee a son also of her: yea, I will bless her, and she shall be mother of nation; kings of people shall be of her. (v. 15-16)

Satan made two attempts to defile Sarah through an

adulterous act, first by king Pharaoh of Egypt our first account in Genesis **_Chapter 12_** and secondly by King Abimelech of the south country of Gerar. Satan created these evil scenarios by operating through the spirit of FEAR AND LYING. Fear and lying have become Abraham's familiar spirits, they know him; while the familiar spirit of lust plagued the King of Egypt and King Abimelech.

ABRAHAM SAID OF SARAH, HIS WIFE, "SHE IS MY SISTER"- _Genesis 20:5._

We know by reading Verse 12 of **_Gen. Chapter 20_** that Sarah actually was his half sister, since both of them had the same father, but we also know that she was infact his wife. Both of them told the King that Sarah was his sister. The same familiar spirits of lying and fear that were operating in Abraham's life in **_Chapter 12 continued_** to operate in his life through **_Chapter 20 and_** they have also influenced Sarah's life.

Do you now understand how these spirits work? When they are acquainted with a person, they lurk around him in order to influence his thoughts and actions. Since they know much about their acquaintances, they understand exactly what it takes to influence them.

They know when and how to make their victims steal, get angry, fornicate, lie, withdraw, be proud; they know how and when to make them give up, quit, attempt to commit suicide and even doubt God's word. Because they are familiar with you, they understand your limitations. Unless you put your trust in the Lord Jesus Christ as your shield and strength, stand on the word of God they will mess you up.

There are some familiar spirits that are common place, they are often called environmental spirits, they are confined to a country, city or town. They are found everywhere they are assigned. You will find for instance around any brothel, motel, discothèque, tea or soup cafe, public beaches in any country whether in the country side or big cities such familiar spirits of sexual perversion, lust, homosexuality, alcoholism, gambling and violence lurking around the places. They know these locations very well and they are familiar with their acquaintances that are patronizing them.

There are likely to be an increasing presence of the spirits of dishonesty, fraud, bribery, divorce, rape, organised violence, gangsterism, prostitution, stealing in commercial or big cities like Lagos, Kano, New York, Chicago, London, Rio-de-Janeiro, Bombay, Rome, Warri or Aba than in the rural areas.

The familiar spirit around casinos, floors of stock exchanges anywhere in the world are that of anxiety, fear and greed. It is also generally known that the most indulged past time of sailors is alcohol gulping and womanizing. The spirits of lust and alcoholism are their acquaintances. Spirits of infirmity and death have heavy presence around hospitals and various morgues all over the world.

WHICH SPIRITS HAVE BECOME FAMILIAR WITH YOU? CAN YOU DISCERN ANY? YOU BETTER GO INTO IMMEDIATE SPIRITUAL WARFARE AGAINST THEM, OTHERWISE THEY WILL MESS YOU UP.

Because they have known you, the earlier you identify them, bind and cast them out of your life, the better for you. They are quite destructive. They perpetuate evil occurrence in one's life. Apostle Peter called them devourers:

> *"Be sober, be vigilant; because your adversary the devil, as a roaring lion, walketh about, seeking whom he may devour"*
> <u>*1 Peters 5:8*</u>

You had better watch out for the attacks of these familiar

spirits, the unseen devils. Get them arrested before they arrest you. They are all over, seeking their acquaintances to destroy or cause sorrow of heart.

A Brother came into our Ministry one day and wanted to speak with me concerning some experiences of sexual immorality threatening his Christian life. He was a highly placed elder in his church. He suddenly realized that within a period of time his appetite for sex outside his marriage has become uncontrollable. Infact he could sleep with any woman at any place, as long as she bears a feminine feature. He became a sex predator, a lawful captive of sexual demons.

Most times after his illicit sex escapades, he would engage on a marathon fasting and prayer, yet he could not overcome this weakness. After counseling, I told him two things will help him out. First, the decision to repent and secondly the FAMILIAR SPIRIT OF ASMODEE who is the satanic prince responsible for sexual perversions must be bound and cast out of his life.

Thank God that after ministering deliverance to him and the sexual perversion spirit cast out of his life, he has enjoyed victory over the sin of adultery. His spiritual life developed very fast and he has since recorded more remarkable successes in his career and Christian life. He is now a director in a top class company.

Unless the strongman (age long familiar spirit) attached to you is bound, and his goods (evil works) are destroyed, you will never enjoy peace and prosperity in your life.

"When a strong man armed keepeth his palace (House), his goods (evil works) are intact."
<u>Luke 11: 21</u>

"Infact how can one enter a strong man's house and plunder his goods, UNLESS he first binds the strong man and then destroy his goods."
Mathew 12: 29

CHAPTER TWO

THE MANIFESTATIONS OF FAMILIAR SPIRITS IN HUMAN LIFE

As earlier said, familiar spirits are evil spirits. They are demons, agents of Satan perpetuating spiritual wickedness in high and low places. They execute the manifesto of their evil kingdom i.e. to STEAL, KILL and DESTROY. Our Lord Jesus Christ exposed them in *John 10;10* "*The thief cometh not, but for to steal, and to kill and, to destroy;* Who is the thief, killer and destroyer? SATAN! He is the number one enemy of man. He heads the kingdom of evil and darkness.

We can easily determine the characteristic of a kingdom from the character of its king. In verses 10 and 11 Jesus told us about His character. *"I have come that they might have life, and that they might have it abundantly. I am the good shepherd; the good shepherd giveth his life for the sheep."* Familiar spirits are all around people, assigned to do satan's evil bidding against mankind. They attach themselves to individuals, families, communities, nations, institutions, races and group of persons in fraternities.

MANIFESTATION BY ASSIGNMENT

A familiar spirit can be assigned to any human being through demonic projections immediately they are born or even in their mother's womb if she is not covered by the blood of Jesus; just as the Holy Spirit can come upon a child right from the mother's womb. Let us go through a biblical account:

__Luke 1:13-15__

> *"But the angel said unto him, fear not, Zacharias, for thy prayer is heard; and thy wife Elizabeth shall bear thee a son, and thou shalt call his name John. And thou shalt have joy and gladness, and many shall rejoice at his birth. For he shall be great in the sight of the Lord, and shall drink neither wine nor strong drink, and he shall BE FILLED WITH THE HOLY GHOST, EVEN FROM HIS MOTHER'S WOMB"*

We can see that the Holy Ghost has been upon John the Baptist right from his mother's womb. Let us also consider the descriptive account of Jacob in *__Genesis Chapter 25:21-26__*

> *"And Isaac entreated the Lord for his wife, because she was barren, and the Lord was entreated of him, and Rebecca his wife conceived. And the children struggled together within her, and she said, if it be so, why am I thus?*
>
> *And she went to enquire of the Lord. And the Lord said to her, Two nations are in thy womb, and two manner of people shall be*

separated from thy bowels; and the one people shall be stronger than the other people; and the elder shall serve the younger.

*And when her days to be delivered were fulfilled, behold, there were twins in her womb. And the first came out red, all over like an hairy garment and they called his name Esau. And after that came his brother out, and his <u>**HAND TOOK HOLD ON ESAU'S HEEL;**</u> and his name was called Jacob.*

    The spirits of contention, strife, deceit and lying had identified themselves with Jacob right from his mother's womb where he was contending with Esau because he wanted to be delivered first.

    The Bible says *"He took hold of Esau's heel"* as they were being delivered and throughout Jacob's life history the spirits of contention and deception became familiar with him. They always lurked around him. He was involved in controversy of deception and cheating first with his brother Esau then his father-in-law Laban who put Leah his eldest daughter in Jacob's arm instead of Rachel to whom Jacob was espoused and for whom he had served a seven-year-term. He deceitfully usurped Esau's birthright. He also wrestled with an angel of God.

    Familiar spirits are also assigned to places especially at their inception. For example, the day a brothel, casino or hotel is commissioned for commencement of business, demons of lust, prostitution, adultery, alcoholism, Asmodee (the prince of darkness responsible for sexual perversion) will be allocated to them. They will attach themselves there to perpetuate evil.

    Immediately a bank is commissioned the spirits of

fraud, stealing, covetousness or greed are assigned to them. They begin to lurk around and get acquainted with the mode of operations in the bank and their staff.

THESE ARE TRUE AND OFTEN UNIMAGINABLE REALITIES!

The churches are not left out. One of the most familiar spirits that operate in churches today is commonly termed "Charismatic Witchcraft". This occurs when a minister of God controls his congregation through fear, intimidation or through other bogus manipulations of the word of God to soothe his whims and caprice.

The charismatic witchcraft spirit is in operation when you have a minister threatening his members who attend other churches after God has blessed them in his congregation. Therefore claiming it will be ingratitude to God for such members to transfer their membership or benefit from other ministries outside his own.

This ungodly act is very common with many ministers of God who have constituted their Churches into personal empires or corporations. It is an irony that those who have been called to be under shepherds (hirelings) by the Lord to feed and nuture the sheep (believers of Christ) are now claiming ownership.

A Christian out of good conscience, in good faith can move to any arm of the Body of Christ without prejudice of Church leadership. No Church leader has right of ownership over any of his member. Where selfish tendencies are translated into wicked manipulations and control of membership of Church, witchcraft spirit will manifest. Beware!

This familiar spirit is also seen manifesting when the minister becomes very autocratic, while none of the elders or members can proffer any genuine suggestion and his words are decrees. This manipulation is also obvious when members especially elders or the diaconate consciously or otherwise, want to control the minister through selfish and ungodly inspirations. Most agents of satan assigned to churches work their ways through the leadership strata and begin to operate witchcraft spirit. They become ready instruments for the devil to destroy churches.

The church is distinctly, preeminently and absolutely a spiritual institution, created, vitalized, possessed and directed by the Spirit of God. Her machinery, sites, forms, services and officers have no comeliness, no pertinence, no power, except as they are dispositions and channels of the Holy Spirit. If the devil can by any method shut the Holy Spirit out from the church he has effectually barred the such from being God's representative institution on earth. Nevertheless, the gate of Hell will never prevail against the church, our Lord Jesus has decreed.

> *The church is distinctly, preeminently and absolutely a spiritual institution, created, vitalized, possessed and directed by the Spirit of God.*

Mammon spirit through another servient spirit called GREED has also taken over many churches, having become their acquaintance. The lust for material wealth, power and money is being glaringly equated to prosperity. Every Christian is made to believe that he is a potential millionaire and "wealthy man".

The churches have been converted into institutes of advanced business studies, we have become too familiar with so many seminars of "how to press buttons" "how to increase your finances" or "how to maximize your opportunities" and seeing less of workshops on how to win souls for Christ and other discipleship training programmes.

The spirit of mammon has blinded the eyes of so many ministers of God and their congregation that they can no longer distinguish between MATERIALISM and PROSPERITY, GODLY LIFE and WORLDLINESS.

Watch out for advert like "how to discover your potentialities in your careers " *"How to create wealth"*. Recently, I saw a church advertising its "Business Academy". God have mercy on us! Satan is unrelentingly trying to ensure that material elements of strength are substituted for the spiritual. This is one of devil's most insidious and successful methods to deceive, divert and deprave the Church through familiar spirits called mammon and greed. The love of luxury is being flamboyantly displayed to prove that "Abraham blessings" are ours.

> *The spirit of mammon has blinded the eyes of so many ministers of God and their congregation that they can no longer distinguish between MATERIALISM and PROSPERITY, GODLY LIFE and WORLDLINESS.*

Another dangerous spirit that has been assigned to so many churches today is what I refer to as the "SPIRIT OF IT DOES NOT MATTER", is also known as the spirit of worldliness. This spirit has deprived so many Christians from living a holy life or being in the right standing with God in their daily Christian living.

The spirit of IT DOES NOT MATTER influences them to believe that holiness is not attainable. So many ministers and Christians believe that whatever they do doesn't matter as long as it is done in the name of the Lord, more so when they are under GRACE and have been declared the righteousness of God in Christ Jesus.

Many have turned Christianity into mere sociality, that's why many churches and Christians have confused ENTERTAINMENT for MINISTRATION, PHYSICAL ENERGY FOR ANOINTING, FACT FOR TRUTH, MORALITY

FOR FEAR OF GOD, not knowing that they are led by the devil. One of the most misunderstood and misinterpreted scriptures to support this mishap is:

> ***2 Cor:3:17b** "Where the spirit of the Lord is there is liberty"*. Apostle Paul warned about the abuse of our liberty in ***Galatians 5:13** "For, brethren, ye have been called unto liberty; only use not liberty for an occasion to the flesh, but by love serve one another"*.

The "SPIRIT OF IT DOES NOT MATTER" has become one of the most familiar and destructive spirits operating against so many churches today. This spirit for example, does not allow the church leadership to check and counsel properly on the way members dress to church.

A sister can dress in a mini-skirt with her under wears almost vulgarly exposed to the church, no female usher would be sent to counsel her, as far as they are concerned, it does not matter after all she is born again and has received the baptism of the Holy Spirit. **GOD WILL SURELY HAVE MERCY ON THE CHURCH, AMEN!**

A brother can defraud his company of huge sums of money or use his public office to cart away millions of public funds, donate part to the church and when such unpleasant acts get to the knowledge of the church leadership with proofs, they wave it off- **"IT DOES NOT MATTER"**, after all it is the Lord that has given us the power to make wealth. Why not! The earth is the Lord's and the fullness thereof, all things belong to God.

Church leaders are afraid to stand boldly on the side of righteousness and Biblical truth to condemn adultery, adulterous and iniquitous marriages engaged in by their followers, even Ministers of God; for fear of been labeled too religious or been prejudicial.

Glamour in Hollywood style in the name of prosperity has been brought into the church, from the pulpit to the church gates. Apostle Paul was amazed at the happenings in the church in Rome and he declared:

> *"Let not sin therefore reign in your mortal body, that ye should obey it in lusts thereof. Neither yield ye your members as instruments of unrighteousness unto sin: but yield yourselves unto God, as those that are alive from the dead, and your members as instruments of righteousness unto God. <u>For sin shall not have dominion over you: for ye are not under the law, but under grace:</u>*
>
> *What then? SHALL WE SIN, BECAUSE WE ARE NOT UNDER THE LAW, BUT UNDER GRACE? GOD FORBID!"*
> <u>*Rom. 6:12-16*</u>

This is the generation of vipers and hypocrites worse than the time of Sodom and Gomorrah, Jesus Christ spoke about. If the generation of Sodom and Gomorrah had the opportunity to hear the truths preached, and the signs performed in our time, Jesus said they would have been saved.

The church lives in a hostile and satanic world. Within and around her are enemies that not only could distract her but also are meant to and will, unless she resists force with a greater force. But because the Holy Spirit rules over the church of Christ then we can shout H-a-l-l-e-l-u-y-a-h! Glory is to God. The church is marching on. The saints have overcome by the blood of Jesus Christ.

MANIFESTATION BY ASSOCIATION

Familiar spirits attach themselves to groups of persons who associate closely. I normally call this "bondage by association". This also brings up the common saying "Birds of the same feathers flock together". It is explained in this scripture:

> *"I wrote unto you in an epistle not to company with fornicators: Yet not altogether the fornicators of this world or with covetous, or extortionist, or with idolaters' for then must ye needs go out of the world. But now I have written unto you not to keep company, if any man that is called a brother be a fornicator, or covetous, or an idolater, or a railer, or a drunkard, or an extortioner, with such an one no not to eat".*
> <u>*1 Cor:5:9-10:*</u>

You will become like your friends and associates. You can be influenced by the association or company you keep. A person or group with strong familiar spirits assigned or attached to them will influence you soulishly and spiritually through your association with them. The spirits of sexual perversion and addictions could influence you if your main companions are prostitutes, club dancers, pornography subscribers.

Your marriage could suffer some setbacks if your very close friends are unbelievers who are gossip monger, divorcees or unmarried persons; even believers who are fornicating and committing adultery delibrately. If casinos have become your second home you will very soon be influenced by the spirit of gambling, alcoholism and sloth assigned to casinos.

King Solomon is regarded as the wisest and richest man that ever lived; God blessed him with wisdom and great wealth. He had more understanding than any man that ever lived, yet his life was almost ruined by evil companionship with hundreds of strange women. He corrupted his wisdom unto acquiring heathen women; he was lured to partake in the worship and sacrifices to their foreign gods. Their familiar spirit of idolatry became familiar with Solomon and he was destructively influenced.

The Bible records that his heart was after their imported strange gods:

> *"But King Solomon <u>loved many strange women</u> together with the daughter of Pharaoh, women of the Moabites, Ammonites, Edomites, Zidonians and Hittites, of the nations concerning which <u>the Lord said unto the children of Israel, ye shall not go in to them, neither shall they come in unto you: for surely they will turn away your heart after their gods: Solomon clave unto these in love.</u> And he had seven hundred wives, princesses, and three hundred concubines <u>and his wives turned away his heart.</u>*
> *<u>1 King 11:1-3</u>*

Let us examine the Holy Ghost influence on Saul in the company of prophets: *<u>1 Sam. 10:5,10</u>*

> *"... And it shall come to pass when thou art come thither to the city, that thou shalt meet a company of prophets coming down from the high place with a Psaltery, and tabret,*

and pipe, and a harp before them; and they shall prophesy, And when they came thither to the hill, behold a company of prophets met him (Saul), <u>and the Spirit of God came upon him, and he prophesied among them".</u>

GOOD ASSOCIATION GOOD INFLUENCE! GOOD SPIRIT GOOD INFLUENCE!

My Friend! Bad companies ruin!! They will turn away your heart from God. Don't tolerate such, they are silent instrument of destruction of your adversary the devil. They are ready tools for familiar spirits to manipulate your destiny.

MANIFESTATION THROUGH FAMILY TIES

Many familiar spirits are linked to families and because of their long acquaintance with such families through generations, they are often called familiar or "Family" spirits. During many counselling sessions I often come across these familiar or "family" spirits afflicting many people including Christians.

As I was counselling a christian sister who has been married thrice to three husbands and divorced thrice before she gave her life to Christ, I noticed that her two elder sisters were experiencing the same marital problem. The first had married twice and divorced; the second, twice and divorced; and her third marriage was about to hit the rocks. She also confirmed that her father had many wives. These are no coincidence, but a satanic trend that was undetected in their family.

By the unction of the Holy Spirit, I was able to discern that the familiar spirit called Abandon working through another spirit Asmodee was assigned to their paternal generation; these two spirits are responsible for unsuccessful marriages, prolonged bachelorhood and spinsterhood and multi - marriages.

They reign in so many families perpetuating evil, and unless they are resisted and arrested by the power and authority of Jesus Christ, many generations of the families to which they are assigned will never enjoy marital blessings.

Have you noticed a young girl whose behavioural pattern is very similar to her mother's, may be her pride or her saucy attitude, her sharp tongue or revengeful temperament? She might also manifest some good sides of her mother. Have you heard people say "she is just like her mother and worse off like her grandmother, in this violent attitudes that she exhibits"?

For a very long time I was unconsciously exhibiting certain bad traits of my father and surprisingly I watched my son who is my first child unconsciously exhibiting the same traits. It took the grace of God through the help of the Holy Spirit for me to overcome them. I also solicited same help for my believing son. These are familiar or family spirits who know both my paternal and maternal family lineages that are still hanging around to continue there age long influences. Except they are quickly discerned and resisted they may perform many destructive jobs in the lives of many.

King David's problem with the familiar spirit of lust and sexual perversion continued to influence his descendants; not only did he have eight wives, he converted one of them (Bathsheba) through adultery and murder. But his son Solomon created a Hebrew record of philandering; he had seven hundred wives and maintained three hundred standby concubines. David's eldest child Absalom slept publicly with David's wife in an adulterous act. Another of his son Amnon raped his own half sister Tamar thereby committing incest. Asmodee, the familiar spirit responsible for sexual sins is just ravaging King David's household unperturbed.

Another amazing case was that of Zacharias the priest of the highest God, the familiar spirit of doubt manifested prominently in his family line. Angel Gabriel conveyed God's message to Zacharias the priest (Minister of God) about his yet to be born child John the Baptist with authority and divine assurance. He embarrassed the angel by asking for a sign to prove the authenticity of the message because he doubted its possibility, considering that Elizabeth and he were very old:

> *"And Zacharias said unto the angel whereby shall I know this? For I am an old man and my wife well stricken in years". And the angel said unto him, "I am Gabriel, that stand in the presence of God; and am sent to speak unto thee; and shew thee these glad tidings. And behold, thou shall be dumb, and not be able to speak until the day these things shall be performed, <u>because thou believest not my word which shall be fulfilled in their season".</u>*
> **(Luke 1:18-20)**

Zacharia doubted God's message and asked for a proof. The sign given to him became a punishment for his unbelief. "HE DOUBTED"

John the Baptist the son of Zacharia began ministry as a forerunner of our Lord Jesus Christ to fulfill the prophecy of prophet Isaiah:

> *"The voice of him that liveth in the wilderness; prepare ye the way of the Lord; make straight in the desert a highway for our God".*
> *<u>(Isaiah 40:3)</u>*

He baptized many Jews and others who cared to believe his gospel in the River Jordan and Jesus came to him to be baptized too. Let's see this account in **_John 1:29-34_**

> *"The next day John seeth Jesus coming unto him; and saith, Behold the lamb of God, which taketh away the sin of the world. <u>This is he of who I said, after me cometh a man which is prepared before me; for he was before me.</u>*
>
> *And I knew him not: <u>but that should be made manifest to Israel therefore am I come baptizing with water"</u> And <u>John record, saying, I saw the Spirit descending from heaven like a dove, and it abode upon him. And I knew him not but he that sent me to baptize with water the same said unto me; upon who thou shalt see the Spirit descending, and remaining on him, the same is he which baptizeth with the Holy Ghost. And I saw and bare record that this is the Son of God".</u>*

Inspite of this impressive public testimony of the messiahship of Jesus Christ, the familiar spirit (family spirit) called the spirit of doubt knew John the Baptist very well, he was very much acquainted with his family; he tormented his father Zacharias and now attached to John. The spirit had been following him everywhere and caught up with him eventually when he was imprisoned by king Herod.

Luke 7:19-23 explains:

> *"Now when John has heard in the prison the works of Christ, he sent two of his disciples. And said unto him* **ART THOU HE**

THAT SHOULD COME OR DO WE LOOK FOR ANOTHER?** Jesus answered and said unto them, go and shew John again those things which ye do hear and see: The blind receive their sight and the lame walk, the leper are cleansed, and the deaf hear, the dead are raised up and the poor have the gospel preached to them. **AND BLESSED IS HE WHOSOEVER SHALL NOT BE OFFENDED IN ME"

Jesus Christ like angel Gabriel was equally embarrassed by John the Baptist who had publicly acknowledged and announced him as the Messiah-Son of God, sending to ask him again for a proof. LIKE FATHER LIKE SON! LIKE ZACHARIAS LIKE JOHN THE BAPTIST! The spirits that influence or control the parent frequently control the children, and many times their manifestation in the second, third and fourth generation are worse than the first.

Family spirits will do their best to become familiar with you, they would want to dominate and control your life. Thank God there is a balm in Gilead! The name and the Blood of Jesus. Each and everyone of these spirits can be cast out of your life and out of your family or from member of closely related groups, if they are quickly discerned through the help of the Holy Spirit.

Babies or children have very little natural or spiritual resistance and it is relatively easy for a spirit especially those familiar with the family to attach to a child or a baby

The familiar spirit (family spirit) called the spirit of doubt knew John the Baptist very well, he was very much acquainted with his family; he tormented his father Zacharias and now attached to John.

christian, unless someone is covering them with prayers.

When you begin to examine individual families or groups who associate closely, you will be amazed to see the same common group of spirits operating in their lives. Fear, envy, pride, alcoholism, rise and fall, rejection, lying, sexual promiscuity, doubts, poverty, delay, unsuccessfulness, suicide etc.

When you see these spirits in operation, understand that they come from the devil. You need also to realize that it is not every problem you have that is caused by familiar spirit inherited through your family lineage or close associates. Some of your problems may be caused by spirits who have just arrived the scene.

Evil spirits don't give up, they are very persistent and become resident around you when they receive very little encouragement, they will become very familiar with you, and begin to dominate your thoughts and actions.

A Christian whose thought life is controlled and submitted to God is open to godly guidance of the Holy Spirit the rest of his life. Everything you do goes by and through your thoughts. Your effectiveness as a Christian is determined by how pure your thought life is. As a man thinketh the Bible says so he is.

Demons gain entry into a human life through undisciplined thought life. They have the supernatural capability to project their influences via the thinking faculty of a person's mind. Apostle Paul in ***Philippians 4:8*** *advised us to be mindful of what our thought pattern should be: "Finally, brothers, whatever is true, whatever is noble, whatever is right, whatever is lovely, whatever is admirable, if anything is excellent or praiseworthy, think about such things".*

Your thoughts are the expressed feelings of your spirit (your inner man) and your spirit operates freely in the spirit realm; this realm is free also for both good and evil spirits to operate. Evil thoughts attract negative and evil manifestation good thoughts are attracted to goodness in the realm of the spirit. MIND YOUR THOUGHTS!

Always endeavor to reject and cast down any unclean and unholy imagination projecting into your mind, especially when such imaginations are against the obedience of the word of God. All temptation begins in thoughts, the devil takes advantage of our thought life to make us sin.

> *Evil thoughts attract negative and evil manifestation good thoughts are attracted to goodness in the realm of the spirit. MIND YOUR THOUGHTS!*

Imaginations are spiritual blocks, as you hold on to an imagination whether negative or positive you are constructing a manifestation.

A sustained imagination whether good or evil is an expectation in the making, and it will eventually become a reality. Holy, righteous and good thinking is good for your spirit, soul and body.

> *"Casting down imaginations and every high thing that exalted itself against the knowledge of God and bringing into captivity every unholy, ungodly thought to the obedience of Christ"*
> *2Corinthians 10:15*

Your mind is the central processing unit of your reasoning, decisions, emotions, thoughts and choices that you make. Keep it safe, renewed and strengthened with the word of God. Your life will follow the direction of your mind.

CHAPTER THREE

FAMILIAR SPIRITS AND THEIR MODES OF ATTACK

We are at war. Mankind is perpetually at war whether we are conscious of this or not. The evidence is all around us. Random order, Rape, epidemics, Drug and Alcohol addiction, Deceit, Government Corruption, Increased rate of Divorce, Fraud, Street Violence, Terrorism, Robbery, Child Abuse, Secret Cults in High School and tertiary institutions of learning, the list of these evils is inexhaustible.

Spiritual warfare is a multilevel conflict between good and evil initiated on the supernatural plane with the prehistoric rebellion of Lucifer and transfer to the natural plane with the fall of man. Satan, man's adversary, continues to work to deceive and divert people from salvation in Jesus Christ, and to harm and hinder Christians through enticement to sin, exploitation of their weakness and perpetual attack on their God given goodness.

Because Satan is the author and initiator of the origin of sin, the god of this world; spiritual warfare involves a constant multidimensional battle against the world-system of ungodly values, the flesh and the devil that is the supernatural personification of evil.

The visible Church has never been free from satanic and demonic opposition surrounded by apathy or hostility, infiltrated with division, legalism, intellectualism, idolatry, and sinful practices. There can be no doubt as to who is behind the wretched-man, poverty, blindness and nakedness which Jesus Christ foretold:

> *"Because you say, "I am rich, have become wealthy, and have need of nothing and do not know that you are WRECTHED, MISERABLE, POOR, BLIND and NAKED" (Rev. 3:17)*

The battle grounds for this war are: The heavens, the human mind and the church. The human mind is made of four sections: THOUGHT, MEMORY, EMOTION AND INTELLIGENCE. They are wonderfully made by God. These four faculties of the human mind and his WILL make up a man's soul. SOUL = MIND+WILL.

Evil spirits attack the human mind in order to gain control of a person's soul; satan blinds the mind of the unsaved (unredeemed) man from the light of the gospel of Jesus Christ:

> *"But even if our Gospel is veiled, it is veiled to those who are perishing. Whose minds the god of this age has blinded, who do not believe, lest the light of the Gospel of the Glory of Christ, who is the image of God should shine on them." (2 Cor. 4:3-4)*

Familiar spirits constantly invade the human mind in three main dimensions of action:

    (i)   INFLUENCE (OPPRESSION)

(ii) DEMONISATION
(iii) OBSESSION

Any of these measures is an oppressive bid to establish a foothold on a human soul in order to manipulate his thoughts, emotions, intelligence, memory and will. **_Proverb 4:23_** warns:

"Keep thy heart (mind) with all diligence, for out of it are the issues of life".

FIVE ENTRY POINTS OF THE HUMAN SOUL

There are five major spiritual entry points or gates by which access could be gained into the human soul: The EYE, EAR, MOUTH, UMBILICAL CORD AND SEX ORGAN. The easiest entry points amongst these are the eye and ear.

The thought compartment is linked with the eye and ear gates, it is the satellite dish of the mind. Through the ear gates it receives or hears sound waves (words); through the eye gates the thought compartment receive pictures (visions and images) which is commonly called imagination or fantasy. What you see and hear helps in constructing your thoughts.

Thoughts are the processed data of the soul. But the words (sound) and images, (things that we see) come externally through the eye and ear gates or internally through the inner voice or dream experience. The external is a conscious act while the internal experience like that of dreaming is a subconscious act.

Satan has masterfully enslaved millions of unregenerated human spirits and influenced many Christians with the spirits of this world through their eye and ear gates. It is a biblical truth that immorality is first committed in the imagination, thus at the thought level before it is committed with the body.

> ***"You have heard that it was said, "You shall not commit adultery". But I say to you, that whosoever looketh on a woman to lust after her hath committed adultery with her already in his heart"***
> ***Matt. 5:27-28.***

Most evil are committed first in our imagination before our deeds. What Jesus Christ tried to emphasize in this scripture is that imagination is an action of the inner man. The feeling of your spirit emanates from deep inner working. Thoughts are inner actions whether good or bad.

INFLUENCE

It is very clear that the battle of the mind is the battle of control. In the ordinary understanding, nobody can forcefully control or manipulate the mind of a person. The choice of who controls is absolutely decided by the person through his will. Mankind has the option to either yield to the Spirit of God or to demons.

The spirits of the world are the familiar spirits; they are evil spirits, which always tend to control the human mind through deceitful and diabolic manipulations to make man sin against God. Whereas the Spirit of God who is the Spirit of truth and love, relates with man through grace by faith in Christ Jesus, and through the word of God.

In ***Ephesians 2:1-5:*** Apostle Paul describes the condition of all men before being made alive by grace in Christ.

> ***"Men are dead in their trespasses and sins; they walk accordingly to the course of this world"*** they live ***"indulging the desires of the flesh and of the mind"*** Men are ***"by nature the children of wrath".***

This is true of all mankind without exception. The unredeemed (unsaved) man is bound to making a wrong choice of who to succumb to because he is in spiritual darkness. He is vulnerable to the attacks of evil spirits, who through deceitful manipulations have kept him in perpetual spiritual bondage if he is not turned from darkness to light by accepting Jesus Christ as his savior.

Believers who do not guard their minds and crucify their flesh will be influenced by their familiar spirits. Whosoever controls the mind of a man actually takes the actions. "Let **the meditation of my heart be acceptable unto you Oh! Lord,"** cried the Psalmist-King David.

DEMONIZATION

There exists a common argument as to whether or not a believer can be oppressed or demonized. The various understanding on this matter have given rise to certain myths and one of such is that "CHRISTIANS CANNOT BE DEMONIZED". This is one of Satan's favorite lies. If he can get the entire body of Christ to believe these lies, demons will work freely undisturbed within many Christians' lives and even churches.

Prominent Christian leaders are exponents of this myth, most of them are victims of rationalization, spiritual pride and to some extent loud ignorance. Many Christians who are against demonization hold on to this fact but thank God that the Holy Spirit has been opening the spiritual eyes of understanding of many so as to avoid being messed up by these diabolical spirits.

Their doctrine assumes that since the Holy Spirit lives

within a Christian, he cannot be demonized, this assumption is unconsciously employed by them when interpreting the Bible and human experiences. They adduce it as a biblical truth whereas in reality, it is not.

It is an unchallengeable truth that a demon cannot live in a Christian's spirit because the Holy Spirit lives there. But when the christian continuously grieve the Holy Spirit, and eventually dine and shakes hand with the devil, Holy Spirit will gently permit demonic operations in the believer's soul and body, Christian thus becomes the house of demons.

Let us examine *1Samuel 16; 14-15, 23*

> *Now the spirit of the Lord had departed from King Saul, and an evil spirit from the Lord tormented him. Saul's attendant said to him, "see, an evil spirit from God is tormenting you. Let our lord command his servant here to search for someone who can play the harp. He will play when the evil spirit comes upon you, you will feel better."*
>
> *Whenever the evil spirit comes upon Saul, David would take his harp and play. Then relief would come to Saul: he would feel better, and the evil spirit will leave him.*
> *1 Samuel 16:14 - 15, 23*

We can understand certain truths from here. Firstly, the Spirit of God that departed from King Saul is the same Holy Spirit that dwells in believing Christians. He can in other words allow the oppression of evil spirits. I mean demonic manifestations. Secondly, it is an unchangeable truth that this present state of Saul's demonization is as a result of deliberate disobedience to God and his blatant show of arrogance.

To obey is better than sacrifice, and to heed is better than the fat of rams. For rebellion is like the sin of witchcraft and arrogance like evil of idolatry. Because you have rejected the word of the Lord, He hath also rejected thee from being king.
<u>*1 Samuel 15: 22b – 23*</u>

Don't forget that Saul is also Abraham's son; he is a covenant child like you. He is a chosen generation, the apple of God's eye. God personally chose him for the office of the first human king of His firstborn Israel. Remember that God told king Pharaoh that Israel is His firstborn. (Exodus 4:22). Yet the Lord still allowed His Spirit to depart from Saul for the reason of SIN. The Bible said SAUL REJECTED THE WORD OF THE LORD.

My Christian brethren deliberate and continuous rejection of God's word will enlist one in the pathway of darkness, and the realm of darkness is the domain of demons; any believer that slides into these satanic premises will suffer demonization. The Bible in <u>*Galatians 6:7*</u> says *"Do not be deceived: God cannot be mocked. Whatever a man sows he will surely reap. The one who sows to please his sinful nature, from that nature will reap DESTRUCTION; the one who sows to please the spirit, from the spirit will reap the blessings of eternal life".*

Though demonization is not always as a result of sin in a person as we may see later in the subsequent chapters; there are different kinds of evil spirits, and not all of them are what I refer to as "spirits of sin". This does not restrict the truth that sin is a huge entry point for demonic influence. For every sin in the Bible there is a corresponding demon. Any Christian living in sin or living in the flesh cannot escape relationship with demons.

Man is made of three parts, Spirit, Soul and Body <u>*(1*</u>

Thess. 5:23); he is a tripatite personality. But there are two kinds of men: the saved (regenerated) and the unsaved (unregenerated man). The regenerated man is the man who accepts by faith that Jesus Christ is his Lord and Saviour and he supernaturally experiences a NEW SPIRITUAL BIRTH - Born Again! The other is the natural man who rejects the salvation of his soul by rejecting Jesus Christ ***John 3:5-7;16-18*** explains this.

The spirit of the believer (regenerated man) is the residence of the Holy Spirit but the unredeemed man is rebellious against the Holy Spirit - he has vacancy inside his spirit for demons to reside. Therefore, a believing child of God cannot be possessed by demon in his spirit unlike the unsaved man who is a ready made house for demons.

Nevertheless, <u>a christian can be demonised as a result of several attacks on his soul through the lust of the flesh, as explained earlier.</u> **The human mind** (soul) of a believer is the battle ground where two ethical forces of the flesh and the Spirit want to impress on.

> *"For the flesh lusteth against the Spirit, and the Spirit against the flesh: and these are contrary one to another. So that ye cannot do the things that ye would".<u>Galatians. 5:17</u>*

Demons may hook up with a person who violate God's laws whether a Christian or unbeliever. Typically, this happens when someone gets involved in the worship of false gods, occult-divination, horoscope, sorcery, spiritualism, holds on hatred towards another person, jealousy, violent anger, practices sexual immorality, or loses control through drugs or alcohol; continously living an unrepentant sinful life.

This kind of demonic oppression can also happen when someone comes into contact with a person or place that may have been demonised by curses, spells, hexes or through violent crime of rape, attempted murder, sexual abuse, or satanic ritual.

A familiar spirit may leave the abuser and attach itself to the victim. <u>Any legal ground given to satan, either through wilful sin, ignorance or unbroken ancestral curses and covenants, if not annulled will certainly provoke demonization of a person whether he is a Christian or an unbeliever.</u>

If you are constantly been oppressed, you may be encountering the influence of FAMILIAR SPIRITS (FAMILY SPIRIT) that found entrance into the blood line of your family at some point. If you are one of the few in your family line who have given their lives to Christ, there may be a river of ungodliness that flows in your life path. It is appropriate to build a spiritual dam to cut off the effect of the devil of the former generations.

A believer who is being oppressed by demons is regarded as the recipient of a demon's action, and by means has lost control over an evil act. The soul of a Christian can be demonised, even ministers of God can be demonized without them knowing it. I have seen many Christians and Servants of God moving around with demons in their pockets like cracker biscuits without them knowing.Only to be manifesting the evil works of these devils. By their fruits not gifts you will know them.

> *If you are constantly been oppressed, you may be encountering the influence of FAMILIAR SPIRITS (FAMILY SPIRIT) that found entrance into the blood line of your family at some point. If you are one of the few in your family line who have given their lives to Christ, there may be a river of ungodliness that flows in your life path. It is appropriate to build a spiritual dam to cut off the effect of the devil of the former generations.*

There is this story of an assistant pastor of a very big church in the United State of America. Listen to his experience:

> "I was the associate pastor of the church", said Rev. John. "It was and probably still the largest and fast growing church in the city. People come to Christ weekly during the church service; Our Senior Pastor TRULY PREACHES THE WORD OF GOD"
>
> One day a young married woman came to me for counselling, she was broken hearted because she had been having an extra-marital affair, God has brought her such conviction that she has already broken off the illicit relationship. I ministered to her from the word of God, assuring her of God's forgiveness and praying with her. Finally, after the session she said, "Pastor, the worst thing about this affair is the person with whom I have been involved is our Senior pastor".
>
> John was speechless. At first he thought the woman was lying that perhaps she was infatuated with the Senior pastor and was out to hurt him because he was unresponsive to her flirtations. But the more he counselled her the more he became convinced of her sincerity.
>
> Over the course of months following this counselling session, several other women came to him (John) the associate pastor with this kind of story. All had been having sexual affairs with the Senior

Pastor. John carefully investigated each case. He had to have irrefutable evidence with which to face his Senior Pastor, because he had a strong personality, and John knew his own ministry was in jeopardy if the Senior Pastor denies the charges. Several of the women were willing to face the Senior Pastor, John and the elders to testify.

To cut this story short, by the time John was to resign his associate pastorship because of the unco-operative position of the Senior Pastor and the elders when he called for an investigation, he had talked with about thirty women with whom the Senior Pastor had sexual relations with over the years. THIRTY WOMEN IN ONE SINGLE CHURCH! HE WAS A SEX PREDATOR.

This of course is not an anointing of the Holy Spirit but a high degree of demonisation. John's Senior Pastor over the years has been demonised by the familiar spirit of lust and Asmodee who is the prince of demons responsible for sexual licentiousness. He needs deliverance ministry urgently otherwise he may break king Solomon's record. A Christian can be demonised.

Over the years I have counselled thousands of spirit-filled believers who have been attacked and hindered by the influence of forces which they could not understand and led them through deliverance ministry. Praise God they have been restored, set free by the Holy Spirit and now living a victorious christian life with success and joyful testimonies to the glory of God.

John's Senior Pastor for example, inspite of his state of demonisation is responsible for his actions, he chose to walk in the flesh in the area of sexual immorality. To sin or not is a matter of choice. Satan is often involved in sin, so are demons. Where SIN FLOWS, demons flow. They thrive on sin because it is their way of life. Familiar spirits are all around to perpetuate the SIN WAR between the flesh and the Spirit in the life of a Christian.

OBSESSION

Obession is a high degree of demonisation, a persistent control of a person by evil spirit. A demonically obessed person is the one who has lost his mind to the demons possessing and controlling him. He has totally lost his personality as a result of his affliction; he can be described as the one who has lost the personal harmony of his soul. The demons that possess him drive and compel him into evil and destructive actions at every least opportunity. Let us consider the story of the demoniac of Gadarene.

> *"And they arrived at the country of the Gadarene, which is over against Galilee. And Jesus went forth to the land, there met him out of the city a certain man which has devils longtime, and wear no clothes, neither abode in any house, but in tombs.*
> *When he saw Jesus he cried out, and fell down before him, and with a loud voice said, what have I to do with thee Jesus, thou son of God most high? I beseach thee, torment me not. For Jesus had commanded the unclean spirit to come out of the man. For often times it has caught him: and he was kept bound with chains and in fetters; and he broke the bands and was driven of the devil into the wilderness".*
> <u>Luke 8:26-29</u>

From these four verses (26-29) we can deduce the following about the demoniac of Gadarene:

(i) He has been possessed by a legion of devils.
(ii) His possession had spanned a long time.
(iii) He was stark naked, wearing no clothes.
(iv) He does not habitate amongst the living, he preferred to live in the tombs.
(v) Often he suffered violent manifestation to the extent of been chained with fetters of iron.
(vi) He often broke off these chains with his physical strength to set himself loose.
(vii) He was driven by the demons from the tomb to the wilderness.

All these manifestations are proofs of an obsessed person who has lost his mind. He has lost his personality; he preferred to live in the graveyard; go about naked; his place of resort is the wilderness. Having made the tombs his residence he will become a ready acquaintance of the demons of death and destruction. He did physically cut off chains with violent eruptions.

ATTACKS THROUGH DREAM

One of the easiest and principal means by which satan and his agents attack people is through their dreams. The dream realm is the soul realm of mankind, this realm is like a free high way for which both the spirits of God and the devil have free access. About seventy-five percent of satanic attacks on man takes place during his sleep.

This is one area many people especially Christians are ignorant of, and have as a result suffered severe misfortunes, marital problems, wretchedness, emotional wreck, disappointments, failures, prolonged bachelorhood or spinsterhood, barrenness, chronic illness, financial losses, frustrations and sorrow of heart to mention but a few. The truth is that when people are deep asleep they are at the lowest level of spiritual energy and that is why deep and excessive sleepers are vulnerable to destructive satanic attacks in their dream state.

Let us see our Lord Jesus' illustration concerning sleep:

> ***"But one night as he slept, his enemy came and sowed tares among his wheat, and went away".***
> ***<u>Matt. 13:25.</u>***

Witches, wizards and other demonic entities are the enemies and they plant evil tares in the lives of many people in their dreams. When I was counselling a twelve year old girl possessed of witchcraft spirit, she confessed that most attacks on their victims were carried out in the dream realm. They afflict people with sickness, diseases and other wickedness through occultic projections in their dreams.

Most often these attacks are carried out through direct manifestations or impersonation. Sometimes they give people food, money, gift, bad news, evil report about other persons, to distract, deceive, obstruct, collect information; to initiate and win people unconsciously into satanic covenants. All these and other multidimensional evils take place in the dream state of man.

There have been several cases of persons, Christians and ministers of God whose sanctity were defiled by demons or other agents of satan by impersonating their spouses, relations, friends, church members or strange personalities to have sexual intercourse with them in their dreams. I have heard of so many people narrating dream experiences of dead relations, friends and other distant personalities appearing to them to have one transaction or the other, some could be friendly and others very antagonistic.

All these impersonations are done by familiar spirits; that is evil spirits taking human forms to relate to you in your dream state. They know you and have information about your life history; your family, ancestors, co-workers, friends, schoolmates, community and neighbours. They know your hometown. They know your brithday and birth place.They have complete dossier of every human being, if you are a Spirit filled Christian they also know.

Satan is very deceptive in the business of impersonation and imitation, this is an area where his kingdom thrives. Deception is one of his highly recognised mode of operation against mankind. So through high occultic powers these familiar spirits can perpetuate evil in the lives of people in their dream. The truth is that those appearing to you as your late father or mother or friends or acquaintance are fake identities, they are being impersonated by demons.

Like we discussed earlier, no dead person has any ability to communicate with the living. Familiar spirits only imitate and impersonate the dead. For the Bible says:

"And as it is appointed unto men once to die, but after this judgement" <u>Heb.9:27.</u>

I have heard so many people say they don't experience dreams whenever they sleep. This is a very dangerous situation. Every human being that sleeps should have a dream experience. Nevertheless, several people often forget their dreams, and when this persists, they ignorantly conclude that they don't have dream experience.

The following is a confession of a former satanist who has repented and surrendered to the saving grace of Jesus Christ: "It is a known fact in the spirit world that human beings can be contacted or reached through their dream which is their soul realm, and majority of Christians are led astray into a backsliding state because we visit them in their dreams to give them food, beautiful gifts and money through high occultic projections. We take them to strange places like forest, schools, church gatherings, rivers to swim in their dreams and unknowingly to our victims they are being unconsciously initiated into mammy water or the marine spiritual kingdom. We do impersonate people who are familiar to them to have sexual intercouse with them through INCUBUS-SUCCUBUS a bisexual demon. Through this evil act, we can project lust waves into the thought realms of our victims, cause barrenness or miscarriage in the women; cause perpetual quarrels between spouses which normally end up in divorce and other marital misfortunes".

"In most cases male victims suffer the same consequences with the female except that they often suffer financial and business set back, while ministers of God are weakened spiritually. Another affliction commonly suffered as a result of this sexual pollution is persistent and often incurable waist pain or unusual heat in the lower abdomen of our victims. We do defile and weaken Christians spiritually beyond their

understanding. We also assign to many, spiritual husbands and wives in their dreams, this will hinder the unmarried from having suitors or experience prolonged bachelorhood or spinsterhood, some may never marry except this marriage with their spiritual concubines (Spouses) is revoked by the power of Jesus Christ".

Every person and animal you see in your dream is a spirit being and you must test the spirit to know who they are, many agents of satan, demons, witches and wizards impersonate masquerades, military and security personnels, snakes, cows, crocodiles, octopus, rats, lions, pimps, giants, cats, madmen, dogs to attack people in their dreams.

For example, you graduated from University ten years ago, it is therefore an evil experience to see yourself in your dream in a classroom of your former high School you graduated from sixteen years ago, writing semester examination. This is backwardness. A premonition of backwardness and stagnancy in your present life endeavours or ministry assignment. God's will for us in the Bible is to have progress and success in life, and to prosper in the works of our hand.

For example, you graduated from University ten years ago, it is therefore an evil experience to see yourself in your dream in a classroom of your former high School you graduated from sixteen years ago, writing semester examination. This is backwardness. A premonition of backwardness and stagnancy in your present life endea-vours or ministry assignment. God's will for us in the Bible is to have progress and success in life, and to prosper in the works of our hand.

The Bible states in **_1 John 4;1_** that we must test every spirit whether they are of God. You can only do this when you are in your conscious state after your dream, by assessing the actions and object of discussions of the spirit beings relating to you in your dream and compare these with the position of the word of God concerning them.

> *Many agents of satan, demons, witches and wizards impersonate masquerades, military and security personnels, snakes, cows, crocodiles, octopus, rats, lions, pimps, giants, cats, madmen, dogs to attack people in their dreams.*

Another way is for you to consider whether the persons these spirit beings are impersonating speak, have same resemblance or act in real life in the very manner of these spirits in the dream, if you are very observant and careful you will spot some differences. If you observe closely you may notice some differences in their personal features or mode of dressing or mannerisms compared to the personalities they are impersonating in your dream.

I had a dream sometimes ago where a familiar spirit was impersonating my late father who died several years ago, when I woke up I asked the Holy Spirit to help me in interpretation. I noticed that the spirit being that manifested in my dream was wearing a bogus moustache and was a bit aggressive, whereas in real life my father before he died never kept a bogus moustache, moreso, he was a non-aggressive complete gentleman. I bind that spirit in Jesus name and destroy every evil communication he established with my soul.

NON-SATANIC SOURCES OF DREAM

However, not every dream is from the devil, there are

good dreams as well, the Bible says every perfect and good gift is from God:

> *"Every good and perfect gift is from above, and cometh down from the Father of all lights with whom is no variableness or shadow of turning".*
> *James 1:17*

Everything God created for man is perfect and to serve a good purpose in his life, so are dreams. But the devil's own plan for man is to destroy every goodness God has for him especially through corruption. Satan does not create, he pretends he does by imitating through corruption of every good and perfect thing God has made. He is a liar, destroyer and deceiver.

God has divinely made dream a spiritual on-line to communicate spiritual information to man for his own goodness.

> *"For God speaketh once, yea twice, yet man perceiveth it not. In a dream, in a vision of the night, when deep sleep falleth upon men, in slumbering upon the bed, then he openeth the ears of men, and sealeth their instruction, that he may withdraw man from his purpose, and hide pride from man".*
> *Job 33:14-17*

We can understand form this scripture verse that God speaks to people in dreams when they are asleep in order to communicate wisdom and instructions that will make them avoid doing evil and warns them of the penalties of sins, and keeping them from falling into some traps of the devil.

God given dreams can relate to the event of the past,

present and future. There are four ways by which one can know if a dream is supernaturally given by God:

> (i). It will not instil fear, worries and anxiety in you, instead you will receive the peace of the Holy Spirit after the dream.

"The Lord will give strength to his people; the Lord will bless his people with peace". Ps. 29:11

> (ii). It's content will not instruct you contrary to the word of God.
> (iii). A God given dream will encourage you; give you a stronger faith.
> (iv). Every action the dream foretold will surely come to pass if you are living in obedience to the commandments of God.

"And the Lord answered me, and said, write the vision and make it plain upon tables, that he may run that readeth it. For the vision is yet for an appointed time, but at the end it shall speak, and not lie: though it tarries, wait for it, because IT WILL SURELY COME TO PASS:. Habakuk 2:2-3

A dream is a kind of vision, it is the vision of the head.

"But there is a God in heaven that revealeth secret, and maketh known to the king Nebuchadnezzar what shall be in the latter days. Thy dream, and the vision of thy head

upon thy bed are these".
Daniel 2:28

Another source of dream is a person's thought. Thus, your conscious mind is being revealed in your subconscious state. Most of the things we thought of previously could show up in our dream, this kind is sometimes called the natural dream.
Isaiah 29:8,; Eccl.5:3 explain this.

"It shall even be as when an hungry man dreameth, and behold he eateth, but he awaketh, and his soul is empty: or as when a thirsty man dreameth, and behold, he drinketh, but he awaketh, and behold he is faint, and his soul has appetite".
For a dream cometh through the multitude of thoughts...."

Thus a dream is either from God, satan or your multitude of thoughts. In the spirit realm positive attracts positive and negative attracts negative. Positive thoughts will result in positive natural dreams, while negative thoughts will result into negative natural dreams. Our thoughts could be reproduced in our natural dreams. You thought about travelling to your home town and saw yourself in your next sleep dreaming about your home town, this is a natural dream.

Dreams are very important. They convey information from the unconscious realm of the soul to us. The soul realm is the dream state of man, and the spirit of man freely participates here. Therefore, dreams bring to our conscious knowledge, activities that have taken place in the spirit realm.

When a dream originates from God or satan it has meaning and should be given attention through interpretation. God has given certain Christians in the Body of Christ the gift of the interpretation of dreams. Every dream from satan will always bring anger, fear, affliction, anxiety, deception and could be relatively contrary to the word of God; they should be prayerfully nullify in Jesus name. God given dreams increase faith in Him, bring joy, enforce God's word and are beneficial to the dreamer.

In a rationalistic society such as ours, spiritual things like dreams and visions are generally regarded with condescending skepticism. That's understandable,for not all men are spiritual; the Bible says spiritual things are for spiritual people. Neither are all of faith. But this attitude is also pervasive within the church as well. The result is to first dismiss dreams entirely since they occur outside of logic and self- control. Secondly, many are taught to view dreams as deceptive and heretical,they often imply that revelation from God rarely occur outside of scripture. This is pure sense knowledge.

The people in the Bible clearly understood and expected that God would speak to them through dreams and visions, and He did it so many times. There are all kinds of doors into spiritual dimensions; dreams and visions are, but two of them.

We must not take dreams as mere frivolities, a man who is careless about his dreams is working in the colony of danger. Many persistent sufferings and frustrations of Christians are as a result of their careless handling of their dreams.

The kind of dream you have, where you have it, the detail of that dream are very sensitive matters. How you handle it when you wake up matters a lot. For example it is very dangerous to eat and have sexual intercourse continuously in your dream experiences.

When a married woman for example, engages in sex in her dream with an opposite sex with the face of her husband or a strange man, everything in her husband will begin to repel her; she will suddenly begin to dislike her spouse and quarrel unneccesarily and nothing he does gives her pleasure, instead she will pick fault with every of his words and deeds. Through this dream manipulation a demon has been assigned to destroy the joy and the peace of her home.

Anytime you have sex in your dream, satanic sexual substances are deposited inside you and this has several times caused infertility in men and women that defy medical solution. Such cases call for fervent prayers of deliverance from Jesus Christ,because the sufferer is in serious satanic bondage.

It is wrong to eat in your dream. Food is not created by God for the soul or spirit but for your body. The only food for the spirit and soul according to the Bible is the word of God. Jesus Christ spoke clearly that man cannot live on physical bread alone but he requires also the word of God which is the spiritual food for his spirit.

Jesus answered, it is written: ***"Man does not live on bread (physical food) alone, but on every word of God (Spiritual food)" Luke 4:4***

>***How sweet are thy words O Lord unto my taste! yes, sweeter than honey to my mouth. Psalm 119:103***
>
>***Thy word were found, and I did eat them.... Jeremiah 15:16***

It is therefore dangerous and diabolical to be eating and drinking in your dream; whereas your physical body is alseep, your SPIRITMAN is busy eating satanic menu.

If you find yourself eating meat or beans in your dream, you are being unconsciously initiated into satanic wickedness and organised destruction; and in your subsequent dreams you will begin to find yourself in the midst of strange people and strange fellowships carrying out deeds that are naturally despicable to you. It will take the mercies and the power of Jesus Christ to set you free.

If you drink coke or eat any palmoil soup or stew in your dream, you are drinking blood through satanic manipulation. All these diabolical food and drinks projected into peoples soul through satanic dream manipulations, are to cause their victims perpertual ill health, sickness and diseases that defy medication, and to finally enslave them into sorrowful experiences of life. Such persons require counselling and deliverance ministration to loose them from bondage.

Many Christians who out of ignorance have been victims of this delibrate satanic manipulation of eating and drinking in their dreams, suddenly begin to find it difficult to read their Bible (Word of God) and to pray. Anytime they attempt to pray or read the word of God, they suddenly experience so much heaviness. Whereas they could spend several hours reading other non-christian titles, magazines and even in television viewing.

Over 80% of the thousands of Christians that have undergone counselling with our ministry had been eating, drinking and having sex in their dream experiences. Many marital homes have been destroyed; many peoples' health have been afflicted; peoples' lives and destinies have ended up in wretchedness because of satanic dreams.

To swim in the river, climb hills; wade through muddy waters; appearing naked, pursued by cows, snakes, masquerades, madmen, violent men, are all satanic dreams to cause the dreamer sorrow of heart and destruction.

What kind of dreams do you have? They all have meanings, consult the ministers of God with the gift of interpretation of dreams or solicit the help of the Holy Spirit. However, every dream that brings fear and sadness to your soul should be immediately nullified prayerfully by the power of Jesus Christ. Act quickly before your destiny is wrecked.

CHAPTER FOUR

FAMILIAR SPIRIT AND MEDIUMS

A medium is a person who consults with familiar spirits by allowing evil spirits to communicate through him to this physical world. Most of them are usually witches, wizards, false prophets, diviners, native doctors, fortune-tellers and necromancers. They enlist the co-operation of familiar spirits and use the tools of the spirit world to draw others into the demonic realm. The witch of Endor in *1 Sam. 28:7* is a good example of a medium.

Mediums are satanist who use devices such as fortune telling, finding lost objects, proffering mystical healings to all kinds of ailments to secure their customers; they also help many of their clients "peep" into their future through ouija boards, palm reading, crystal balls, oracles, horoscopes, levitation, prophecies, mind reading, telesthesia or tarot cards. Consulting through oracles is a very common practice in the third world nations especially in Africa, Asia, South America and the Caribbeans. God warns his chosen people to always shun mediums:

> *"Regard not them that have familiar spirits neither seek after wizards, to be defiled by them: I am the Lord your God"* **Lev.19:31**
>
> *"And when they seek familiar spirit, and unto wizards and witches that "peep" and mutters, should not a people seek after God instead?"* - **Is. 8:19** *(Amplified)*

A young man came to me sometimes ago, he had been having some rough times in life, nothing seemed to be working right for him, his cycle of misfortunes, unsuccessfulness continued unabated. When I asked him what the matter was he hastily replied "I want you to help me check my future". I looked at him straight into his eyes and discerned that he was not a Holy Spirit filled Christian. He was an unbeliever. I told him I am not a medium or a spiritist prophet and infact he was in the wrong place. I told him he needed Jesus Christ in his life to be sure of his future. He immediately apologised and went out of my office.

It is an old time practice for people and nations to try and get secret or hidden knowledge, especially of the future by consulting mediums, oracles, spiritist prophets and prophetesses. It is biblically wrong for Christians to try to know or have a peep into their future. God's chosen people can enquire from Him concerning a matter through prophets of God and in the dispensation of the church of Christ, Christians go to their ministers or directly enquire from the holy scriptures or the Holy Spirit. Prophet Isaiah emphasised the danger of consulting mediums - **Isa.8:19**

Moreso, Jesus Christ made it possible for the children of God to have direct access to the throne of God to seek His face concerning any matter. It is scripturally wrong and also an act of unbelief for any Christian wanting to peep into the future of his destiny. Once a person accepts Jesus as his

Lord and Saviour, then his future is secured in Christ Jesus, especially when he continues in obeying God's commandments. Obedience to God's commandment enables the enrichment of His blessings in a Christian's life. Moreover, the eternal future of the saints is peaceful and very glorious.

"For I know the thoughts that I think towards you, saith the Lord, thoughts of peace, and not of evil, to give you an expected end". Jeremiah 29:11

Many who consult mediums always defend their actions, claiming that there is nothing wrong with spiritism and have often put the following defence:

i. It has been a long time practice of their ancestors, families, tribes or culture.
ii. There have been proofs of correct forecasts from these mediums, their verdicts concerning life matters have been accurate.
iii. They are rendering good services, helping people out of their problems.
iv. There are indications to show that they are not suffering any harm as a result of their consultations.

Nobody is questioning these facts but the word of God remains absolute truth, we must obey God's commandment strictly. God is God. He is Almighty and all knowing. Omniscience! Once He says we should not, we must not!

"There shall not be found among you any one that maketh his son or his daughter to pass through the fire, or that useth divina-

> *tion, or <u>an observer of times,</u> or <u>an enchanter</u> or <u>a witch,</u> or <u>a charmer,</u> or <u>a consulter of familiar spirits</u> or <u>a wizard</u> or <u>a necromancer.</u> For all that do these things are an abomination unto the Lord: and because of these abominations the Lord thy God doth drive them out from before thee"* <u>Deuteronomy 18:10-12</u>

It is very clear from God's commandment if you indulge in these practices, you are an abomination unto God. What becomes of the person who is an abomination unto God? He will be eternally separated from God if he does not repent and will be an instant prey for the devil to destroy. Remember satan's manifesto in <u>*John 10;10*</u>

"to kill, to steal and to destroy". This is his ministry as far as every mankind is concern.

If you are a consulter of mediums you have readily opened an entry port for demons into your life, and be assured that you will be thoroughly messed up in every affairs of your life. Obey God's commandment and enjoy His blessings, disobey and incur the consequences. The choice is simply yours.

THE DECEPTIVE ROLES OF FAMILIAR SPIRITS

Many persons have been deceived by the role of familiar spirits operating through mediums such as soothsayers, witch doctors, spiritist prophets and prophetesses, oracles or fortunetellers because of the accuracy of their divinations. Like I have explained earlier, the accuracy of foretelling is not proof of guarantee of genuineness of the foreteller.

This is clearly seen in <u>*Acts.16:16-18*</u> where the slave girl who followed Apostle Paul and Silas shouted **"These men are servants of the most High God are telling you the**

way to be saved" yet she was a medium though saying the right thing and closely imitating the genuine apostles of God. She was possessed by the spirit of divination.

Remember familiar or family spirits know the life and family history of the person they are assigned to right from their date of birth. These family spirits are agents of satan and they are assigned to families as communication links. Immediately they are assigned to a newly born child they keep record in files, books, computers and other recording devices ***Rom. 1:20*** says we can have some understanding of the spiritual from the natural. Just as we keep records of events naturally so it is also done in the spirit realm. It is also a biblical fact that there are books and records in heaven.

> *"They that feared the Lord spake often one to another and the Lord hearkened, and heard it, and a book of remembrance was written before him for them that fear the Lord and that thought upon his name: Mal.3:16*

The Bible also spoke about the book of life and the book of judgement ***(Rev. 20:12).*** These recordings of information concerning human beings are done through supernatural manifestations. The spirit realm is more real than this physical world.

When a person consults any medium such as a native doctor or spiritist prophet or a fortune-teller, the familiar spirit assigned to him will link up with the spirit possessing the medium, they will pass very accurate information concerning their assignee to the medium and these evil spirits will now communicate them back through the native doctor, false prophet, fortune-teller to the person who is consulting.

For example, if the familiar spirit attached to MR.

FOLA is the spirit of premature death and FOLA now consults a native doctor or a satanic prophet, this spirit of death will link up with the FAMILIAR SPIRITS possessing the native doctor or fortune-teller and release every information concerning MR. FOLA'S life history to him and warn him through the native doctor against premature death.

Mediums are not genius, they are only privileged to have access to information concerning their consulter who are ignorant of this great occultic deception through familiar spirits. The accuracy of their divinations and forecasts should therefore not deceive people from the truth that they are agents of the devil.

THE CONSEQUENCES OF OCCULT INVOLVEMENT

The occult has multitude of activities in which people consciously or unconsciously become involved. This is quite a vast and complex area which we would not delve into, but the following could be classified scripturally as occult activities.

(i) Consultation with mediums.
(ii) Horoscope patronage.
(iii) Divination.
(iv) Membership of secret societies.
(v) Necromancy and sorcery.
(vi) Withcraft practice.
(vii) Unconscious initiations into witchcraft in the dream.
(viii) New Age Movement membership.

Any one that consults a medium or practices any form of occultism opens a door way for demonic afflictions. Immediately a person submits to a spiritist prophet, native doctor, astrologer, palm reader, sorcerers etc. he has willingly solicited for the service of demons. Whether the person directly did the consultation or delegated somebody on his behalf, the deal with the demons have been struck.

Moreover, nothing is free with the devil, a price must be paid for the services rendered by these satanic agents and when this exchange is completed, demons automatically enter into a contract or more committedly a covenant with the person who came seeking their services. Such contract or covenant gives demons easy access to the life of the consulter to cause more serious havoc in his life.

Normally, Christians are protected so that demons cannot get them or oppress their soul, non-Christians also to some extent enjoy God's protection from allowing demons into their lives. But an unrepentant and wilful sinner opens a doorway for demonic manipulation.

Playing with your daily horoscope, the curiosity to consult a spiritist prophets or fortune teller, belonging to secret cults and unholy fraternities, praying with spiritist "special candles" or "holy water", "special soaps" and incenses are enough to affect the rest of your life. At first there may be no evidence of demon's presence but as months and years pass, the demons will begin to manifest their evil works in the life of the consulter of medium or occults practitioner.

> *A lady who claimed to be a Christian came to me with an eight months old child who was delivered with some strange physical abnormalities. The child was looking like a monkey facially, with his hands and fingers abnormally structured. She had this child after many years of difficulties of child bearing. When I asked her where she and her husband visited last outside a minister*

of God to find solution before her pregnancy, she claimed to have consulted a native doctor who specialised in assisting women to get pregnant. The Holy Spirit told me, that was the source of the child's problem. She admitted to have received portions of concotions to drink and underwent some massage rituals from the native doctor. This child was demonised when he was at the foetal stage and she is now suffering the consequences of dining with the devil. A native doctor is the minister of satan.

Mediums are agents of the devil no matter any good solution they proffer, they are deceptive and destructive. They cannot give anybody a lasting joy. Only Jesus can help you.

Isaiah 47:13-15 explains:

"Thou art wearied in the multitude of thy counsels. Let now the astrologers, the stargazers, the monthly prognosticators, diviners, witch doctors, stand up, save thee from this calamity, they shall be as stubble and the fire shall burn them: they shall not deliver themselves from the power of the flame: There shall not be a coal to warm at, nor fire to sit before it. Thus shall they be unto thee with whom thou has laboured, even thy merchants, counselors (Mediums) from thy youth: they shall wander every one to his quarter and none shall save thee".
(Amplified)

NONE CAN SAVE EXCEPT JESUS!

NONE CAN HELP YOU EXCEPT JESUS!!
ONLY JESUS CAN DELIVER YOUR SOUL FROM
CAPTIVITY!!!

> *"But thus saith the Lord, even the captives of the mighty shall be taken away, and the prey of the terrible shall be delivered: for I will contend with him that contendeth with thee and I will save thy children".* <u>Isaiah 49:25</u>

There is no secured future or deliverance with the devil or his agents; those that transact with them will be ashamed at the end, remember also that with the devil nothing is free, if he gives you a chicken he will demand for a cow from you. Woe! to those who will be their consulter.

Now that we have understood the importance of the source of power we solicit help and deliverance from, then how can we identify that which is right? Let's see:-

> *"If there arise among you a prophet, or a dreamer of dreams, and giveth thee a sign or a wonder, And the sign or the wonder come to pass, whereof he spake unto thee, saying, Let us go after other gods which thou hast not known, and let us serve them; thou shalt not hearken unto the words of that prophet, or the dreamer of dreams: for the Lord your God proveth you, to know whether ye love the Lord your God with all your heart and with all your souls"* <u>Deuteronomy 13:1-3:</u>

Therefore, all one needs to do is ask the practitioners to tell him who Jesus Christ is and ask him his relationship with Jesus, if he claims to believe in Jesus Christ as the Living God who came to the world in flesh to die and redeem his soul and trusting Christ as his Lord and Saviour, then you should be assured of dealing with a believer. Whereas, if the practitioner begins to hesitate or talk about other gods, living or dead spiritual masters or speak blasphemous things about the Holy Spirit, you are absolutely dealing with an agent of satan.

Another sure way given by Jesus Christ for us to identify false prophets or spiritualist inspite of their spectacular display of miracles and signs is by their fruits. That is their way of life. Their actions personified. *Jesus said "by their fruit you shall know them". (Matthew 7:17-23)*

CHAPTER FIVE

CURSES AND COVENANTS

Ancestral spirits which are often known as generational or family spirits are basically familiar spirits. They know every family that they have been attached to over generations. They understand every thing concerning members of such families. As generations pass away, they remain in the family to perpetuate multidimensional evils, execute unbroken curses and covenants incurred by forefathers and ancestors. Ancestral spirits are demons; they do not die. They are also called the spirits of inheritance.

A covenant is a formal agreement between two or more persons or parties that is legally binding. These agreements are mutually entered into because the terms and conditions are normally defined. Covenants are made either with God, people or with satan.

There are so many biblical accounts of covenants between persons, between God and individuals, between God and families and the nation of Israel. Let us see:

1 Sam.18:3
"Then Jonathan and David made a covenant, because he beloved him as his own soul". This was a love covenant

between Jonathan and David. God made covenant with men, and Noah was the first to enjoy this priviledge.

> *"And I will establish my covenant with you; neither shall all flesh be cut off anymore by the waters of flood, neither shall there more be a flood to destroy the earth".* <u>*Gen. 9:11*</u>

In <u>Gen. 15:18</u> God made a covenant with Abraham." *In the same day the Lord made a covenant with Abram saying, unto thy seed have I given this land, from the river of Egypt unto the great river, the river Euphrates".*

Covenants could be entered into knowingly or unknowingly and in which ever, it is legally binding. Ignorance is no excuse. Once a person is covenanted he is subject to all the inherent conditionalities. The following are the most common ways by which covenants could be knowingly and unknowingly entered:

(I)   ILLICIT SEX (fornication or adultery),
(II)   INVOLVEMENT IN CULTURAL ACTIVITIES,
(III)   OATH TAKING,
(IV)   BLOOD RELATED SOLEMNITY,
(V)   OCCULT INVOLVEMENT,
(VI)   DREAM EXPERIENCE,
(VII)   BUSINESS AND SOCIAL ASSOCIATIONS,
(VIII) INHERITANCE,
(IX)   IDOLATRY PRACTICES.

COVENANT AND GENERATIONAL LINK

Covenants could span generations especially those made with God, satan or with people where it is so stated, therefore if any of our fore-fathers or ancestors were once involved in any of the aforementioned practices, the consequences which are often multidimensional will spill across the second, third and forth generations except they are discerned and broken by the power of Jesus Christ.

Every covenant God has made with a person, families or the nation of Israel is that of peace, protection, security and prosperity. God also made everlasting covenant with all living creation, the nation of Israel and believers through Jesus Christ. Let's consider:
Gen. 9:16; 2Sam. 23:5; Ex. 31:16:

> *"And the bow shall be in the cloud; and I will look upon it, that I may remember the <u>everlasting covenant</u> between God and every living creature of all flesh that is upon the earth".<u>Gen 9:16.</u>*

> *"Although my house be not so with God; yet he hath made with me <u>an everlasting covenant</u>, ordered in all things, and sure: for this all my salvation, and all my desire, although he make it not to grow". <u>2Sam. 23:5.</u>*

> *"There the children of Israel shall keep the sabbath, to observe the sabbath <u>throughout their generations, for a perpetual covenant</u>" <u>Ex. 31:16.</u>*

God's covenant always have time dimension that span generations especially up to the fourth, unless it is simply stated as an everlasting one,

> *"And I will establish my covenant between me and thee and thy seed after thee in their generations for an everlasting covenant, to be God unto thee, and to thy seed after thee"*

God's plan is a family plan, he always work by covenant with the human race. His covenant of blessings span generations. Let's see *Ex. 34:7.*

> *"Keeping mercy for thousands, forgiving iniquity and transgression and sin, <u>and that will by no means clear the guilty; visiting the iniquity of the father upon the children, and upon the children's children, unto the third and to the fourth generation".</u>*

The devil always like to copy God; he prefers to work also by covenant. Covenant made with satan is usually promising on the surface but the bottom line is that it will lead finally to destruction. The devil is a trickster, the father of all lies. Our lord Jesus exposed him as the one that truth cannot be found in. Satan is the originator of lies and falsehood; he deals with man through deception. Therefore, to make a covenant with him is to choose an easy way to self destruction, very few come out safe and unscathed after the annulment of their covenants with him.

Another terrible thing about him is that he does not create but instead imitates, corrupts and destroys. He is not a wisdom originator but a wisdom corrupter. So many have ignorantly fallen victims of his manipulations and antics, even Christians. Only those Christians whose trust is in the word of God and have good knowledge of the evil devices of Satan have been able to escape from his corrupt and evil schemes.

Many people have been lured to enter into covenant with him because of his promises to give them MONEY, PROTECTION, POWER, AUTHORITY AND PROSPERITY, yet such promises end up as misfortunes, premature death and mysterious calamities.

As earlier said, satan likes copying God, so his covenants with people also span generations. If your forefathers and ancestors have entered into covenants with him, the consequences will spill across future generations and descendants. God is a covenant keeping God, so also the devil keeps covenants with people; he does not forget or break them. **_In Psalm. 89.34_** God declared His position concerning His covenant with other parties; this time it was with king David.

> *"My covenant will I not break, nor alter the thing that is gone out of my lips. Once I have sworn by my holiness that I will not lie unto David".*

GOD IS A COVENANT KEEPING GOD! SO IS OUR ADVERSARY THE DEVIL! HE ENFORCES COVENANTS MADE WITH HIM.

Unbroken covenants with satan will bring disaster, destructive consequences into the life of the person and his future generations.

One day we were ministering deliverance to a former occultist who has surrendered his life to Jesus Christ, he had been in the occult for over twenty years. He became very violent as demons were speaking through him. They were saying **"we shall kill him for trying to break our** *covenants"*. The demons said "we". It means they were more than one. They were making a lawful claim over this brother. They knew if the convenants are broken he will be free and cease to be their lawful captive. After several hours of ministry, the demons were subdued and were cast out in Jesus name, this man began to enjoy peace which has eluded him for many years. Any one that is convenanted to satan automatically incurs multiple curses.

BASIC STEPS YOU CAN TAKE TO BREAK YOUR COVENANTS:

(i) Acknowledge your sins, the sins of your forefathers and ancestors, confess them, ask for forgiveness from God through Jesus Christ.

(ii) Accept and confess your belief in Jesus Christ as your Lord and Saviour, that He is God who came to the world in human flesh.

(iii) Renounce every agreement with satan, declare every connection you have with the power of darkness broken in Jesus name, identify any area of your life where you are linked with satan, renounce it and disconnect your spirit, soul and body from him in Jesus name.

(iv) Evacuate every property of the devil in your possession: remove charms, amulets, occultic books, rings, soaps, incense, photographs, artworks, insignia of membership of occult, fraternities, brotherhoods and other materials. They should be sent to a minister of God for burning. Let us consider *Acts 19:18-19*

> *"And many that believed came, and confessed and shewed their deeds. Many of them also which used curious arts brought*

their books together, and burned them before all men: and they counted the price of them, and found it fifty thousand pieces of silver".

(v) Revoke every legal ground that the devil has established to afflict your life as a result of a covenant; mention the individual areas of your life, marriage, business, finances, health where you have suffered satanic afflictions and annul his legal rights. Decree that he must not cross the spiritual boundary Jesus has made around you with His blood.

"As the mountains are round about Jerusalem, so the Lord is round about his people from henceforth even forever"
Psalm 125:2

(vi) Bind and cast out of your life any demon assigned by satan to execute any covenant in Jesus name.

(vii) Declare every covenant you have entered into knowingly or unknowingly or through ancestral lineage to be revoked and renounced in Jesus name. Declare that only the new covenant with God through the Blood of Jesus Christ now operates in your life with power and authority.

CURSES

Curse can simply be defined as prayer or invocation for harm or injury to come upon someone; evil that comes as a response to a recompense. Curse is the direct opposite of blessing.

NO CURSE WITHOUT A CAUSE: The Bible tells us in ***Proverb 26:2*** that a curse cannot be inflicted on a family or an individual without a cause; whether it is calamity, mental disorder, financial bankruptcy, sickness, barrenness, prolonged bachelorhood, poverty, prolonged spinsterhood, premature death or misery, they are all off shoots of a curse.

A curse is an evil consequence, a negative recompense of a cause:

> *"As the bird by wandering, as the swallow by flying, so the curse causeless shall not come".* <u>Proverb 26:2</u>

A curse requires a cause to manifest, and curses are prime entry points for demonic activity. Curses provide legal grounds for satanic agents to afflict human beings with sorrows of heart, destruction and even death.

The following are indications of Curses:
1. Continuous mental, emotional and physical breakdown.
2. Sickness and Infirmities that have defied medical solutions.
3. Hereditary Sickness.
4. Broken Marriage and family splits.
5. Prolonged poverty and unsucessfulness.
6. Being accident prone.
7. Prolonged barrenness and repeated miscarriages.
8. Frequent deaths in families especially premature ones.
9. Unabated cycle of disappointment and failure.
10. Prolonged bachelorhood or spinsterhood.
11. Repeated experiences of uncompleted project.
12. Always been pursued by masquerades, snakes, cows, violent men, carnivorous animals and mysterious wind in the dream.
13. Unabated poverty and wretchedness.
14. Continuous experience of satanic dreams.

15. Prolonged stagnancy in life.
16. Rising and falling in life endeavours.

A curse generally emanates from an enemy and without doubts, our principal enemy is satan, he does not want anybody created by God to be happy, healthy, secured or prosperous and ultimately will stop anyone from getting to heaven. But God is love. He loves mankind and would bless those whom He loves. To those who are saved and born again, He has a special relationship through Jesus Christ. He is their Eternal Father. His fatherly nature is to bless His children with His goodness.

> **Ps. 3:8**
> *"Salvation belongeth unto the LORD: Thy blessing is upon thy people".* **Deut. 23:5b** *"But the LORD thy God turned the curse into a blessing unto thee, because the Lord thy God loved thee".*
>
> **Deut. 28:15** *"But it shall come to pass, if thou wilt not hearken unto the voice of the LORD thy God, to observe to do all his commandments and his statues which I command thee this day, <u>that all these curses shall come upon thee, and overtake the</u>"*

Disobedience to the commandments of God is the fundermental cause of a curse. Everytime a person disobeys the word of God, a legal ground is provided for the devil and his agents to inflict a curse upon the offender. Sin hands over a person to satan the bondmaster, and he hands them over to his agents who are his taskmasters to inflict a curse. A curse does not stray into somebody's life except there is a cause, thus, a curse is a recompense for the disobedience of

God's commandment:

> ***Lamentations 3:64-65***
> *"Render unto them a recompense, Oh lord, according to the work of their hands. Give them sorrow of heart, thy curse unto them."*

TYPES OF CURSES

These are five types of curses:
(1) Curses brought on by disobedience to God's commandments, such as having false gods or other idolatry practices ***Ex. 20:3-4 (Deut. 27:15).*** Disrespect for parents ***(Deut. 27:16).*** Anyone who rebuilds Jericho ***(Jos. 6:26).*** Those who are guilty of certain sins ***(Deut. 27:15-26;28:15-68).***

(2) Curses brought on by the servants of satan e.g witches, native doctors, occultist, spell casters.

(3) Curses brought on by men representing God.
In 2 King 5:27. Elisha the prophet of God places a curse on his servant Gehazi *"the leprosy therefore of Naaman shall cleave unto thee and thy seed forever . And he went out from his presence a leper as white as snow"*

(4) Self imposed curses are those that people pronounced on themselves consciously or unconsciously such as:

> *"I know I will not make it", Nothing I do ever succeeds". "I wish I were dead", Everything is working against me".*

Example of self imposed curses in the Bible are in

(Matt. 27:24-25; Gen. 27:12-13).

(5) Curses brought on by people with relational authority, e.g. parents over children. For example if a father tells his son "you are too sluggish you will never make it in life"

CURSES AND GENERATIONAL LINK

Curses like covenants have generational links or consequences. Where the rebellion against God's commandment is committed by an authority figure especially forefathers or ancestors, the consequences spills over generations from the second and unto the fourth. Let us see *Ex. 20:5* .

> "Thou shalt not bow down thyself of them (false gods) nor serve them: for I the Lord thy God am a jealous God, visiting the iniquity of the fathers upon the children unto the third and fourth generation of them that hate me."

The worship and trust in other gods except Almighty God is iniquity. God is a God of justice and whatever He does is done in righteousness. He has declared He will recompense the iniquity of the fathers unto the bosom of the children. The devil is aware of God's word concerning the sin of idolatry and whenever this commandment is breached, he will invoke a curse upon the offender and his future generations simultaneously.

God is a God of justice and whatever He does is done in righteousness. He has declared He will recompense the iniquity of the fathers unto the bosom of the children.

We can now understand where inheritance comes in the matter of curses. Thus, curses can be inherited from our forefathers or ancestors who have hitherto disobeyed the commandments of God. What *Ex. 20:5* implies is a deliberate turning away from God; usually, if not always, it involves serving other gods or occult involvement, denying God the love and obedience which His singular and absolute Lordship demands.

God passed a divine judgement on the Israelites who were twenty years and above for murmuring against him, He also recompensed their iniquity unto the bosom of their children: *"But as for you, your carcases, they shall fall in this wilderness. And your children shall wander in the wildernesses forty years, and bear your whoredoms, until your carcases be wasted in the wilderness"*
(Number 14:32-33).

> *A young Christian lady came to our ministry sometime ago complaining of an unending cycle of misfortune and disappointment concerning her securing admission into a University or Polytechnic, inspite of her excellent performance in the entrance examinations and requisite qualification. She had prayed, fasted, undergone so many counselling sessions with several ministers of God to no avail. As I was counselling her the Holy Spirit implored me to ask her about her father's religious background, because her problem was that of an inherited curse. This lady told me that her father is a witch-doctor. A witch-doctor is satan's servant, his activities will incur multiple curses for his children; and as his*

daughter, if these curses are not revoked she will ignorantly remain in bondage. One week after deliverance ministry when the ancestral curses were revoked and broken she secured admission into a polytechnic. Praise God!

In *2 King 5:27* prophet Elisha place a curse not only on Gehazi his servant but also on his future generations. *"The leprosy therefore of Naaman shall cleave unto thee, and unto thy seed forever: And he went out from his presence a leper as white as snow".* We can see that Gehazi's curse will be inherited by his descendants. Those involved in satan's service have a good understanding of the importance of heritage, when they place a curse on families they are sure to include all their descendants in the curse.

THE LAW OF INHERITANCE

We would appreciate the reality of curses and convenants and their generational consequences on human lives by understanding the spiritual truth call the law of inheritance. When God made man, He had family in mind. God is a family man. That is why He is called FATHER by His children. So when God created man He created him as a family person, that is why He created him in His own image and likeness.

"So God created man in his own image, in the image of God he created him; male and female he created them". (Genesis 1:27)

God is distinctively three personalities in one; God the Father, God the Son and God the Holy Spirit. They are one God. Man who is created in the likeness of God is also three in one. Inside the first man created was a female called Woman; and inside the Man and the Woman is a child who is the third arm of the family. Inside Adam was Eve, and inside Eve and Adam were children Cain, Abel, Seth and others.

Woman came out of Man according to the word of God in the Bible, and inside the loins of both of them came the children of the family.

> *"So the Lord God caused the man to fall into a deep sleep; and while he was sleeping, he took one of the man's ribs and closed up the place with flesh. Then the Lord God made a woman from the rib that he had taken out of the man, and he brought her to the man.*
>
> *The man said, "This is now bone of my bones and flesh of my flesh, she shall be called woman, for she was taken out of man".*

God was the first person to pronounce a blessing in the Bible, this is stated clearly in Genesis Chapter One Verse Twenty Eight. *Gen. 1:28*

> *"God blessed them and said to them, be fruitful and increase in number; fill the earth and subdue it. Rule over the fish of the sea and the birds of the air and over every living creature that moves on the ground."*

When these blessings were bestowed on both Adam and Eve, their children who were unborn inside their loins were inherently partakers of these blessings. This is the **PRINCIPLE OF INHERITANCE.**

In **_Genesis 3:6-19_**, God was the first person to pronounce a curse, also all the curses He placed on Adam and Eve were automatically inherited by Cain, Abel, Seth and other members of the human race uptil now through their biological blood line. Christians whose faith are in Jesus Christ enjoy a new inheritance in Christ because they are now partakers of the divine nature of Christ by grace. They are God's children through Christ. The next time God openly blessed a person again according to scriptures was upon Noah and his sons (children) saying:

> *"And God blessed Noah and his Sons, and said unto them, Be fruitful and increase in number and fill the earth"* **_Genesis 9:1_**

It is this same God Almighty exercising the principle of inheritance here. The next person after Noah God openly blessed again was Abraham. Not only was he blessed, his children by God's divine decree were also partakers of the blessings.

> *"No longer will you be called Abram, your name will be Abraham, for I have made you a father of many nations. I will make you fruitful; I will make nations out of you, And kings will come from you. **_I will establish my covenant As an everlasting covenant between me and you and your Descendants after you for the generations to come.........".***
> **_Genesis 17:6-8_**

God's covenant of blessings with Abraham simply included his yet to be born children and future descendants. God added a new dimension to the principles of inheritance, thus, not only does children inherit their parents' blessings they also inherit their covenants and curses. This is God's laid down pattern that has not changed.

Even in the New Testatment dispensation it is still much in practice; God has given everyone that believes in Jesus the power to become sons (children) of God and also bequeathed them an everlasting inheritance in Christ Jesus that was legalised through a blood covenant. This is called the NEW COVENANT.The only good news is that God did not bequeathed the believers in Christ any curse; he instead redeemed them from the curse of the law through Jesus Christ.

Satan is a copycat. He does not originate anything except SIN, he appreciates God's unrivalled awesome wisdom and he is an eminent scholar in the study and application of universal spiritual laws. All he does is to imitate God's universal laws and principles; corrupt them to deceitfully lure human beings' loyalty to himself and in a subtle way make them sin against God.Satan exercises the law of inheritance very discreetly whenever he has legal access to people's life.

Unless you locate the source of your problem you will not be able to dislocate it.

Therefore, not only are blessings and covenants inherited from ancestral lineage, curses are often family inherited. These are the consequences of the sins especially the iniquities of foreparents. The Bible says God is not a respecter of persons and He cannot be mocked, therefore whatsoever a man sows he shall reap. The Law of inheritance implies that the children and future generations of a man will likely partake in the reaping of his iniquities

"The Lord is slow to anger, abounding in love and forgiving sin and rebellion. Yet he does not leave the guilty unpunished, he

punishes the children for the sin of their fathers to the third and forth generation".
(Numbers 14:18)

When God placed multiple curses on the son of King Jehoiakim of Judah called Coniah, he included his descendants to fulfil the Law of inheritance:

"This man coniah is like a discarded broken dish. He and his children will be exiled to distant lands. O! Earth, Earth, Earth! Hear the word of the Lord! The Lord says: record this man as childless, <u>for none of his children shall ever sit upon the throne of David or rule in Judah, he shall not prosper in his days; for no one of his children shall prosper"</u>
(Jeremiah 22:28-30)

A Christian sister came to me for counselling sometimes ago concerning her prolonged unemployment after several years as a University graduate. During counselling session, I discovered that her family has the history of nobody becoming successful or prosperous; they suffer a generational curse of unsuccessfulness and disappointment. She has prayed and fasted, attended series of crusades and break through seminars to no avail. During the deliverance ministry by the power of the Holy Spirit we discerned the familiar spirits responsible for the evil and commanded them out of her life in Jesus name. Three weeks after she ended her deliverance she received a letter of employment to commence work with a top American oil producing company with a fantastic salary. Jesus set her free from ancestral curse bondage within few days.

Unless you locate the source of your problem you will not be able to dislocate it.

ANCESTRAL SPIRIT THE EXECUTING AGENTS

Sin is a serious matter with God, He hates it, the devil is also serious about sin, infact he thrives where sin exists. Moreso, sin gives him a legal entry into families to afflict them.

Satan has a sophisticated information network system, and other monitoring devices, he also uses human agents and demons as communication links for information gathering. He thus, possesses a complete dossier on people, families, institutions, communities, nations and even churches. Some of these dossiers on families span many generations.

Ancestral spirits are the familiar spirits assigned to families, they keep record of curses incurred and covenants entered into by these families over generations. They are assigned to execute multidimensional evils as a result of unbroken curses and covenants. Many of the problems which plague mankind such as emotional disorder, mental disorder, alcoholism, unsuccessfulness, marital problems, sexual perversion are not necessarily genetic; suspect a generational curse and ancestral spirit at work if you discover these in both someone being ministered to or in past generation of that person's family.

KING DAVID'S PROBLEM WITH "SEXUAL LUST" INFLUENCED

Absalom, Solomon, Amon and most of his descendants. The generational spirit of sexual perversion operated down David's family line. The idolatry of Jeroboam, son of Nebat cursed his sons. Let see *I King 14:9-10* where God instructed prophet Elijah to deliver a message of judgement to Jeroboam for his sins.

> *"But hast done evil above all that were before thee: for thou has gone and made thee other gods, and molten images, to provoke me to anger, and hast cast me behind thy back: therefore, behold, I will bring evil upon the house of Jeroboam..."*

> *Sister Kemi (not real name) is a believing Christian, married with children but there was no success and prosperity recorded in her life for so many years. All God promised her as her covenant blessings were never manifesting in her life. Inspite of marathon prayers, fasting, intercessions and litres of anointing oil poured on her head to incur God's mercy, nothing changed. Her situation remained the same.*

> *Somebody directed her to our ministry. During my counselling session with her, the*

following facts were established:

(1) She is the first child of her father.
(2) Her father was the first child of her grandfather.
(3) Her grandfather was an IFA-PRIEST.
Ifa - is a satanic idol worshipped by many nations in West Africa, the Carribean Countries, South America especially Brazil, some part of the United States and Cuba. This idol originated from the Yoruba land of Nigeria.

(4) Every first born in the lineage of an Ifa-priest is dedicated before and after birth to the Ifa-god.

(5) As her father's first born she was taken to the Ifa shrine in her hometown when she was still in her mothers womb during her conception to be dedicated, and she was infact dedicated, with all the required rituals.

During our ministering of deliverance prayers to her, a demon spoke and screamed in a very loud voice through her saying: "<u>I am Lucifer I will not let her go because she has been dedicated and covenanted to me when she was in her mother's womb. Why do you want to drive me away now?</u>" I commanded the "Lucifer" spirit to keep quiet and pack out of her life in Jesus name.

> *I revoked that old covenant she has with him, super imposed and over ruled with the new covenant sister Kemi has with God through the Blood of Jesus Christ. She manifested violently and laid lifeless on the ground.*

Sister Kemi was set free by the Spirit of God and today she has new experiences of the abundant life in Christ. She was a victim of ignorance of the Law of inheritance.

Throughout her thirty six years of unbroken ancestral covenant and curses, satan had legal access to plunder God's goodness and blessings in her life. She was a lawful captive of the devil.

There are multitude of Christians groping in the same ignorance especially those from families that have idolatry background. So what about you? Have you taken time to examine your ancestral background, to find out if satan is having a field day disturbing you and your family because of a legal right he holds over you as a result of an inheritance that was passed on to you?

ANCESTRAL CURSES ARE REAL!

Let us see Job's reaction to this truth in **_Job 21:19-21:_** *"God stores up a man's punishment for his children, let him repay the man himself, so that he will know what it is. Let his own eyes see his destruction, let him drink of the wrath of the Almighty for the evils he has done and the curses incurred. For what does he care about the family he leaves when his life span is ended"* (Amplified).

Many are suffering a lot today because of the unbroken family curses and covenants inherited from their unrepentant, ungodly parents or ancestors whose hearts were evil towards God. Some of them were murderers, alcoholics, whoremongers, slave masters, witchcraft and occult practitioners and even satanic priests. They shed innocent blood and perpetuated wanton wickedness. Their hearts were rebellious against Almighty God. They chose the way of destruction.

> *Then the word of the Lord came to prophet Elijah: Go down to meet Ahab King of Israel, who rules in Samaria. He is now in Naboth's vineyard, where he has gone to take possession of it. Say to him "this is what the Lord says: Have you not murdered a man and seized his property? Then say to him, "This is what the Lord says: In the place where the dogs licked up Naboth's blood, dogs will lick your blood - yes, yours!*
>
> *When Ahab heard these words, he tore his clothes, put on sackcloth and fasted. He lay in sackcloth and went around repentantly in regrets. Then the word of the Lord came to Prophet Elijah: Have you noticed how Ahab has humbled himself before me? Because he has humbled himself*
> " <u>**I WILL NOT BRING THIS DISASTER IN HIS DAYS, BUT I WILL BRING IT ON HIS HOUSE IN THE DAYS OF HIS SON**</u>"
> <u>**(1 King 21: 17-19; 27-29)**</u>

Not only do people inherit curses from foreparents, they also inherit good things: Let's see **_2 Timothy 1:5_**

> *"I have been reminded of your sincere faith, which first lived in your grandmother*

> *LOIS and in your mother EUNICE and I am persuaded, now lives in you also"*

Timothy inherited the gift of faith from her mother Eunice through her grandmother Lois, thus his maternal lineage. Not only will present generations benefit from the godliness and righteousness of their fore-parents and ancestors; they will be held responsible also for their iniquities. Let us see the Lord Jesus' remark:

> *"That the blood of all the prophets which was shed from the foundation of the world may <u>be required of this generation, from the blood of Abel to the blood of Zechariah</u> who perished between the altar and the temple. Yes I say to you <u>it will be required of this generation". (Luke 11:50-51)</u>*

Although this injunction was made to the Jews, it automatically applies to non-Jewish nations, tribes and families on earth. The principle remains unchanged, to the Jews first before the gentiles. God always comes to the Jews first:

> *"He came to His own (Jews) and His own (Jews) did not receive Him.*
> *But as many (Gentiles) that received Him, to them He gave the power to become children of God, to those who believed in His name. <u>(John 1:11-12)</u>*

> *I am not ashamed of the gospel of Christ, for it guarantees salvation for everyone who believes, FOR THE JEWS FIRST AND THEN FOR THE GREEK.*
> *<u>(Romans 1:16)</u>*

Let's see how this account explains it:

> *And Noah began to be a farmer and he planted a vineyard,*
> *Then he drank of the wine and became drunk, and he became uncovered in his tent.*
> *And HAM the father of CANAAN saw the nakedness of his father, and told his two brothers outside (did not cover him).*
> *But Shem and Japheth took a garment, laid it on both their shoulders, and went backward and covered the nakedness of their father. Their faces were turned away and they did not see their father's nakedness,*
> *So Noah woke up from his wine and knew what his younger son (Ham) had done to him*
> *Then he said:*
> *"cursed be Canaan (Ham's Son)*
> *A servant of servants*
> *He shall be to his brethren."*
> *(Genesis 9:20-25)*

We can see that the curse was not placed on Ham the offender but on Canaan his son. The guilt of the father passed unto the son. This is the divine pattern. It will never change. Whether you believe or not. Divine truth is absolute.

SIN THROUGH ANCESTRAL LINEAGE

Can sin be inherited? Yes! Sin is an internal and external action of the soul that works contrary to God's commandment. Every descendant of Adamic race possesses a sinful nature which is often termed the nature of flesh. This nature of flesh gives people certain spiritual genetic ability to indulge in any kind of sin that is traceable to parental or ancestral lineage, be it alcoholism, sexual immorality, pride, anger, rape, lying, stealing, violence or murder, just to mention a few.

These sins can also be practiced by individuals or families through transference of spirits. These of course are family spirits which have been hanging around families from generation to generation. Many persons including Christians have shown traits of inherited sins which have passed through their ancestral blood line.

What is commonly understood today is the medical acceptance and proof of genetic diseases and sicknesses but many Christians have not understood the truth that certain sinful acts and afflictions could be "spiritually genetic." For example if you carefully find out, people who were born by parents, grandparents or great grandparents who:

(i) Fornicated before marriage
(ii) Were not legally married

are often likely to be involved in sexual sins before and after marriage. They do also suffer marital problems such as marrying more than once and failed marriages.

If you were conceived by your mother through fornication or adultery, sexual demons will be transferred to you. Let's look at Lot, Abraham's nephew and his descendants.

Now the firstborn said to the younger,
31."Our father is old, and there is no man on the earth to come into us as the custom of all the earth.
32."Come let us make our father drink wine and we will be with him <u>that we may</u>

preserve the lineage of our Father."

33. So they made their father drink wine that night. And the firstborn went in and lay with her father, and he did not know when she lay down or when she arose.

34. It happened on the next day that the firstborn said to the younger, "indeed I lay with my father last night; let us make him drink wine tonight also, and you go and be with him, <u>that we may preserve the lineage of our father."</u>

35. Then they made their father drunk the wine that night also. And the younger arose and lay with him, and he did not know when she lay down or when she arose.

36. THUS BOTH THE DAUGHTERS OF LOT WERE WITH CHILD BY THEIR FATHER.

37. The firstborn bore a son and called his name MOAB, and he is the father of the Moabites.

38. And the younger, also bore a son and called his name "Ben-Amin"; he is the father of Ammon to this day. <u>(Genesis 19:31-38)</u>

The Moabites are biological children through **<u>ANCESTRAL INCEST.</u>** Biblical history shows that they were responsible for the most sexual seduction in Israel's history.

1. Now Israel remained in Acacia Grove, and the people began to commit harlotry (sexual recklessness) with the women of Moab.

> **2. They invited the people to the sacrifice of their gods, and the people ate and bowed down to their gods.**
> **_(Numbers 25:1-2)_**

Not only were the Moabites afflicted by the "genetic demons of sexual immoralities" which have been pervading their generations through ancestral connection. They were biological descendants of incestuous great grandfather (Lot) and grandmother (Lot's daughter).

Not only were the Moabites vast in sexual immoralities they were prominent idolaters who seduced the Israelites into eating the sacrifices of their gods and bowing down to them. In _I Kings 11:1-8_ the same Moabite women led King Solomon astray through inter-marriage and adultery. The Bible said that King Solomon loved Moabite women who were "mobile temples" of Asmodee, the principal demon of sexual immorality.

In the Bible the Ammonites never fared well. They were a sexually depraved nation; a people highly possessed of sexual demons and notable idolaters. They shared unique similarities with their cousins the Moabites. The generational spirits of sexual immorality and idol worship that followed their ancestral parents from Sodom and Gomorrah to the Mountain village of Zoar perpetuated sexual sins in both the Moab and Ammon nations.

God was so angry with them that He banned them from coming near the congregation of His people. They were an abominable nations. Perversed nations of sexual iniquity.

> **_An Ammonite or Moabite shall not enter the assembly of the Lord, even to the tenth generation none of his descendants shall enter the assembly of the Lord._**
> **_(Deuteronomy 23:3)_**

A Christian lady came to me sometimes for spiritual counseling and possible deliverance ministration. In the course of our discussion she mentioned the fact that she has the ability to see some strange "visions" and have premonitions of things before they happened.

By the grace of God I was able to discern that she was a recipient of unctions emanating from the SPIRIT OF DIVINATION, which was an ancestral spirit attached to her family. The Holy Spirit implored me to ask her about her grand father's faith or religious background. I discovered that her paternal grandfather was a voodoo priest - a conjurer and enchanter. Though the grandfather was deceased, the spirit of divination continues to hang on to his descendants and she is one of the inheritors.

Who are your parents, grand parents or great grand parents? You better find out. You will be surprised you have some traits of their sin nature. Try and search for your family history or trace your family tree up to at least three generation's back. Look for your brothers, sisters, uncles, aunties, cousins, nephews, nieces within the span of three to four generations of your family, you will definitely discern a generational spirit or common sin, if you are honest to yourself.

Parents who are involved in sin open the door for demons to attack their children. Demons attachment start very early in life and attempt to build upon foundation through active sin as the child grows into adulthood. But salvation at an early age will destroy much of the enemy's plans for the child's life.

Sometimes ago I was in a church in California in the United States of America to conduct revival meetings, during altar call a sister came out sobbing profusely. After one-on-one counseling, I found out that she was hurt in her heart because her only son who was just eighteen years old was an alcholic and also hooked on drugs. I also discovered that she (the mother), the boy's father, and grandfather were sometimes alcoholics. Brethren, don't be deceived, this is a case of transference of spirit. I mean a case of "genetic sin" in the lives of people.

Many Christians are ignorant of this truth which the Holy Spirit continues to highlight in the church today, and they suffered a lot of sorrows. Ignorance, I mean ignorance of Spiritual truth is very destructive. Come out from among them.

CHAPTER SIX

BELIEVER'S AUTHORITY

THE COSMIC CONFLICT

We cannot have an extensive understanding of believer's victory over satan without an understanding of believer's authority under Jesus Christ. Many Christians still object to the reality of the "Two-Kingdoms - in-Conflict" teaching. One thing I have understood about the word of God is that truth is constant whether people believe it or not. The word of God is truth. Jesus is the word of God. Jesus is truth.

> *"In the beginning was the Word, and the Word was with God, and the Word was God. He (Jesus) was with God in the beginning............, the Word became flesh (Jesus) and dwelt among us. We have seen his glory, the glory of the one and only begotten who came from the Father, full of grace and truth"* <u>John 1:2, 14</u>
>
> *I am the way, the truth*..................<u>John 14:6</u>

The New Testament describes the Christian life as a spiritual warfare. Apostle Paul emphasizes this fact by admonishing us: *"Put on the whole armor of God, that ye may be able to stand against the wiles of the devil. For we wrestle not against flesh and blood, but against principalities, against powers, against rulers of darkness of this world, against spiritual wickedness in high places:* **(Ephesians 6:11-12).**

Scripture abounds in references to such a spiritual conflict, which is to be waged against an evil, cunning, wicked, powerful adversary who rules over a vast and highly organized kingdom.

The reality of the warfare between the kingdom of God and satan can be explained from the several levels of warfare. The first is the prehistoric and ongoing conflict between the Creator and his faithful angels on the one side, and the rebellious hierarchy of evil forces under satan on the other. Though the Bible does not say exactly how angels and demons battle. Perhaps the experiences in Daniel the Tenth Chapter between angel Michael and the prince of Persia could give us insight to this ongoing warfare. The book of Job also reveals a rather formal cosmic interaction between God and satan.

BELIEVERS COMBAT LEVEL

The second level of spiritual warfare is the battle between the demonic clan and the redeemed children of God. **Genesis 3:15** is most foundational for understanding spiritual conflict, it provides a prophetic description of this conflict.

> *"And I will put enmity between you and the woman, and between your offspring and hers; he will crush your head, and you will strike his heel".*

God has divinely proclaimed hatred between sons of men and the seed of the serpent. Until Christ will return in glory and power as a conquering king with his angels to rid the universe of evil men and demons, the devil will continue to "strike at the heel" of the body of Christ, yet the gate of hell will never prevail against it.

This warfare is on. As far as you have the Spirit of God inside you, you are an enemy of satan. Prepare for war! Ready to be tempted, troubled and be attacked. In this war, believers are called the soldiers of Christ who are to fight a good fight of faith. This war is primarily targeted by satan to destroy the faith of believers and their God given blessings.

SATAN'S POWER

Praise God! Let the creation of God praise and magnify him forever. Oh Yes! Satan is powerful but no reason for you child of God to panic because he is only a creation of God. What a marvelous comfort and confidence God gives his children in allowing to see that we need not fear satan. What are his magnitude of power before you child of the most high God? Only God is all powerful.

> ***"God has spoken once, twice I have heard: that power belongs to God." Psalm 62:11***

When satan was chased out of Heaven, God did not remove the power He gave to him as a covering Cherub, his power is not self-originated, the Lord God Almighty deposited it in him. ONLY God is OMNIPOTENT. Power is the righful attribute of God alone.

HOW MUCH AUTHORITY DOES SATAN HAVE?

First and foremost we should understand that the power

satan has was given to him by God. It is a derived power, it is not by right but by permission from Almighty God. Whether in the heavens, the earth or underneath the earth, Jesus told us in *(John 10:10)* what satan wants to do: To steal, to kill and to destroy. He does whatever he can within the parameter of his limited authority. This authority to an extent according to *(Hebrew 2:14,)* include the ability to bring to death, still within the permissive will of God.

From Job's story in JOB the First and Second Chapter, we can make the following deductions:

First, Satan's authority is limited by God, he operates only under the permissive will of God; because of the special protection of God on Job's life, his family and properties, satan could not exercise his evil authority upon him. Infact, if it was possible within his power, satan would have destroyed the entire human race in one moment because of the enormous hatred he has for mankind.

Secondly, under certain circumstances, God grants greater authority to Satan than is ordinarily his. We can see that after the cosmic argument between God and him, God gave him express authority to afflict Job. Then satan answered the Lord, and said:

> *"does Job fear god for nothing? hast thou not made a hedge around him, around his household, around all his properties? You have blessed the work of his hands, and his possessions have increased. But now stretch out your hand and touch all that he has and the will surely cause you to hide your face. And the Lord said to Satan, "Behold all that he has is in your power; only do not lay hands on his life".*
> *(Job 1:9-11)*

We can conclude that Satan does not have enough power and authority to do all he wants at will, nor does he have God's permission to use all the power he possesses. Though his evil desires are boundless not only concerning earthly matters but also in heaven itself. His fondest wish is to dethrone God and set himself in the sacred places of the most high, and to make all creations worship him. But he cannot have this desire accomplished because of his limitations. He has lost out forever.

USING YOUR GOD GIVEN AUTHORITY

Our authority and power as believers is synonymous with our relationship with Jesus Christ. This authority gives us the ability to use the power God has given us through the indwelling of the Holy Spirit in us.

> *"But you have received the Holy Spirit and He live within you, in your hearts,............"*
> *(I John 2:27)*

Most of us, however, seem only vaguely aware of how much power that is, it would be better and profitable if every believer understands and appreciates the truth, that when the Holy Spirit dwells within us, we are invested with the power of God himself and with the full authority of Jesus Christ to use it. It is a great tragedy that many of God's chosen people,

Most of us, however, seem only vaguely aware of how much power that is, it would be better and profitable if every believer understands and appreciates the truth, that when the Holy Spirit dwells within us, we are invested with the power of God himself and with the full authority of Jesus Christ to use it.

although given both His power and authority through His son Jesus Christ, either do not realize what is theirs or else refuse to exercise those rights.

In my ministry I have come across so many former satanists who had been converted to Christ. Many said while they were in bondage of satan they had the occultic ability to "see" with their spiritual eyes the amount of spiritual power different human beings carry with them, and could spot Christians "a kilometer off" by simply noting the amount of power they carried. They all agreed that Christians wield more spiritual power than unbelievers and even satanists but most Christians have no idea of what to do with their God given power. So, such Christians were no threat to them, except those who knew how to use **THE POWER OF CHRIST.** The satanists tried to stay away from such.

The Bible speaks so much about the indwelling power of Christ in Christians: *"Greater is he that is in you than he who is in the world" (1 John 4:4)*

> *"Now, unto him who is able to do, exceeding, abundantly above all that we ask or think, according to the mighty power of God that is at work within us". (Ephesians 2:20)*

MIGHTY POWER OF GOD WORKING WITHIN US!

Christians must appreciate their God given authority and power over *"all the power of the enemy" (Luke 10:19.)* If you are a believer in Christ, rejoice. You have authority over the power of darkness. Never doubt this. Don't confuse this authority with your feelings because your spiritual authority is a legal one delegated to you by Jesus Christ, it has nothing to do with your feelings, thoughts and personality. It has nothing to do with your personal physique, whether you are tall or short or whether you are mature or baby Christian. It has nothing to measure with your academic or racial background, as far as you have the Spirit of Jesus Christ indwelling inside you, you automatically have the legal divine power and authority over all power of darkness.

Nevertheless, satan, your enemy will do everything he can to keep you from becoming convinced of your authority and making you believe your authority is not a reality but mere expression of feeling. Resist this!

In *(Mathew 28:18)* Jesus declared *" I have been given all authority in heaven and on earth "and I have given you (believer) authority so that you can overcome all the power of the enemy" (Luke 10:19.)* Earlier before this declaration, Jesus has given the disciples power and authority to drive out all demons and to cure diseases in *(Luke 9:2,)* this is a clear delegated authority with accompanying responsibility.

The concept of authority is closely related to that of power in the Bible. In the New Testament most especially, the Greek words representing what Jesus gave to his followers are **DUNAMIS,** which means power, and **EXOUSIA,** authority. This God-given authority to a Christian is a gift, it is not earned. It is bestowed to every member of God's family; it is not an exclusive priviledge of personalities but rather it is located in our position as member of God's family.

Are you a believer of Jesus Christ? Do you have the Spirit of God indwelling in you? Therefore, relax and be confident that you have been gifted with the power and authority of God. Do exploits for His kingdom!

This power is given by the Holy Spirit to enable us live a victorious, holy and fruitful life; be a faithful Christian in the Love of God and our neighbors. Also to resist the devil and destroy his evil works of darkness.

Spiritual power and authority are not meant to be kept dormant but useful for our good, the edifying of the Church, goodness of mankind and to the glory of God.

CHAPTER SEVEN

BINDING AND LOOSING

The herald of Christ, His kingdom and the people of His kingdom provoked great expectation in the minds of many people of old time because it was an eternal mystery. People of the old in Bible times, especially prophets of God through divine inspiration of the Holy Spirit gave insight into the womb of eternity.

> *For the earnest expectation of creation eagerly waits for the manifestation of the sons of God.*
> *Romans 8:19*

The people of God, called by His name, for His glory, born of His Spirit not by human instinct, to demonstrate His love, power and grace.

Who are these sons of God? How will they manifest the magnitude of God's love, power and grace; also handle the corresponding responsibilities? Jesus himself offered the answer:

(a) Those that believed in me GREATER

WORKS WILL THEY DO when I go to the FATHER.
John 14:12

(b) Those that BELIEVED IN ME: all these signs will manifest through them. In my name they will CAST OUT DEVILS, SPEAK WITH NEW TONGUES. They will TAKE UP SERPENTS; if they DRINK ANYTHING DEADLY IT WILL BY NO MEANS HURT them, they will LAY HANDS ON THE SICK AND THEY WILL RECOVER
Marks 16: 17 – 18

Brethren! We are not a gang of people seeking political, social or religious identity. We are not a mafia, set up to annex or protect economic and political interests. We are the supernatural children of God empowered, and directed by the Holy Spirit to:

(i) Bind and kick out devils
(ii) Heal the sick
(iii) Proclaim the salvation of God
(iv) Declare the glory of God
(v) Walk in perfect love
(vi) Demonstrate the awesome power of God by working miracles, signs and wonders.

We are by no means ordinary people. We are Sons of God. Children of the Most High God. Extraordinary people assigned to do extra ordinary things.

As a child of God you have been commissioned to extend the kingdom of Christ to every corner of the earth which lies under the control of the wicked one Satan himself. This assignment is not a cheap one. It is a confrontation. The kingdom of light versus that of darkness captained by the ENEMY, our adversary.

Jesus knew the magnitude of this confrontation. "I send you as a sheep amongst the wolf", He warned. He understood the restlessness, evil capacity, and manifesto of Satan's camp to steal, to kill and to destroy. Jesus the good shepherd will not want any of His sheep to fear the evil ones of this world, even when they "walk through the valley of the shadow of death". He made adequate provision for their empowerment. Nobody confronts the devil with boxing gloves. Our assignment is to destroy his evil works.

THE KEYS OF THE KINGDOM

AND I WILL GIVE YOU THE KEYS OF THE KINGDOM OF HEAVEN, AND WHATEVER YOU BIND ON EARTH WILL BE BOUND IN HEAVEN, AND WHATEVER YOU LOOSE ON EARTH WILL BE LOOSED IN HEAVEN.
<u>*Matthew 16:19*</u>

Keys here denote authority. A peculiar and unique authority. Jesus states here in this scripture verse, that the church will be empowered to continue in the privileged responsibility of influencing the earth with His kingdom power and provision.

Jesus is passing on to every Christian His authority TO BIND and TO LOOSE on earth. What a great power and privilege bestowed on every true believer in Christ. This is one of the greatest authority heaven has ever given to mankind. A great divine ability given to us brethren freely by grace.

BINDING

In a broader and more encompassing sense, binding means: restricting or forbidding a person or persons in their freedom of action, choice, expression, to suffer them from any ability of manifestation; It means further, to thwart or frustrate Satanic actions.

LOOSING

The basic meaning of loosing is to untie; to release; to cancel; to free from bondage. Thus freeing a person or persons from circumstances; people from the devil, things that restrict their freedom of action, choice, manifestation of their blessings

The keys of the kingdom are the authority Christ gave believers to exercise the power of the kingdom to bring to pass on earth the kind of effects that takes place in heaven. The key to bind and loose link heaven and earth together, it is the power to accomplish the will of God on earth

My friend, it is the will of God for you as His child to bind and loose, because there are things that need to be bound or loosed. You must restrict, I mean forbid on earth those things that are restricted or forbidden in heaven, and liberate or set free on earth those things that heaven wants to be set free. Have understanding that the earth according to God's eternal purpose, is an extension of heaven. God wants the will of heaven to be done here on earth.

Jesus asked us to pray that God's will in heaven be done on earth. Please get this understanding and let this truth be registered in your spirit. UNLESS YOU BIND AND LOOSE certain things; suffer or release some spiritual manifestation, certain will of God could be hindered from manifesting in your destiny.

By this great power to bind and loose, if someone is BOUND BY SIN, the church which you are a part can "LOOSE" him by preaching the provision of freedom from sin in Jesus Christ:

> **_Romans 6:14_** _says "sin will no longer be your bond master because you are not under law, but under grace offered to you through your faith in Christ"_

If someone is possessed, oppressed, depressed by a demon, you can "BIND" the demon and command his departure from the stronghold he has over the person's life. Many Christians have not utilized this great authority given to them. To bind familiar spirits operating against their lives in diverse manifestations, either as result of their ignorance or resentful attitude about the truth of demons' existence and diabolical operations in the lives of Christians.

The power to bind and cast away devils is a rare grace given to the sons of God who are indwelled by His Spirit. The people of the old covenant time in the Bible did not enjoy this very rich privilege Christ gave us. Moses, Job, Abraham, David, Daniel, Samson, and even Elijah who performed great wonders, had great exploits, were not given the authority to bind devils.

Because Christ had not come in their time, the victory over Satan on the cross had not been accomplished. There was no powerful blood as the BLOOD OF JESUS that they could appeal to overcome the devil. The Bible says we overcome Satan by the BLOOD OF JESUS. Only those who have overcome by the blood of Jesus can BIND AND CAST OUT THE DEVIL.

Let us see this Biblical explanation:

> *Then some of the itinerant Jewish exorcists took it upon themselves to call the name of the Lord Jesus over those who had evil spirits, saying. "We adjure you by the Jesus whom Paul preaches."*
>
> *Also there were seven sons of Sceva, a Jewish chief priest, who did so (exorcise evil spirits in Jesus name).*
>
> *And the evil spirit answered and said. "JESUS I KNOW, AND PAUL I KNOW, BUT WHO ARE YOU?" The man in whom the evil spirit was, leaped on them, overpowered them, and prevailed against them, so that they fled out of that house naked and wounded.*
> <u>Acts 19: 12 – 16</u>

The following truths are herein established in this account:

(i) Only Jesus and His disciples like Paul can bind and cast evil spirits.
(ii) In the spirit world the name of Jesus Christ is highly honored and must be bowed to.
(iii) Those that are Jesus Christ disciples like Paul and true believers in Jesus worldwide are recognized by evil spirits in the satanic world as having authority to bind and cast them.

(iv) No human being without the authority of Jesus Christ can bind or cast away devils. Most times necromancers, exorcists, charmers, pretend to do so, but the truth is that they can only appease devils. None of them can bind and cast out Satan.
(v) It is now a confirmed truth that familiar spirits know you; "Jesus I know, and Paul I know" the evil spirits exclaimed.

It is our divine responsibility to BIND AND CAST DEVILS OUT. Binding and loosing is a "righteous war" every Christian must fight. It is a special spiritual warfare weapon given to all Christians.

It is Satan's strategy to bring every human conflict to a violent confrontation, which results in as much destruction and death as possible. Just as Jesus was sent to destroy the works of the devil, we have been sent into the world with this same commission.

The Bible recorded that the ministry of Jesus was very much involved in binding and loosing through various methods, whereby the works of Satan were destroyed and multitudes were delivered from bondage, and they appreciated God's kingdom, giving God all the glory.

Let us see this Bible account:

> *Now Jesus was teaching in one of the synagogues on the Sabbath. And behold there was a woman who had a spirit of infirmity for 18 years, and was bent over and could in no way raise herself up.*
> *But when Jesus saw her, He called her and said to her "woman you are loosed from your infirmity"*

And he laid hands on her, and immediately she was made straight and glorified God. But the ruler of the synagogue (parish pastor) answered with indignation, because Jesus healed on the Sabbath; and he said to the crowd, "There are six days on which men ought to work; therefore come and be healed then, and not the Sabbath day"

Then Jesus answered him and said, "Hypocrite! Does not each one of you on the Sabbath loose his ox or donkey from the stall, and lead it away to water it?"

"So ought not this woman, being a daughter of Abraham, whom Satan has bound, for eighteen years, be loosed from this bond on the Sabbath?" and when Jesus said these things; all his adversaries were put to shame.
<u>Luke 13: 10 – 16</u>

Let us consider these few truths from this account:

(i) The woman was bent for 18 years she can not stand up straight.
(ii) She was afflicted by the devil called "spirit of infirmity".
(iii) This affliction is equated to have BEEN IN BONDAGE by Jesus.
(iv) Jesus said it was Satan who kept her in bondage; therefore infirmity is the destructive work of Satan.
(v) This woman is a daughter of Abraham, "A covenant child of God".
(vi) Jesus said she deserved to be "LOOSED" from BONDAGE. This is

DELIVERANCE.
- (vii) Abraham's children like Christians can be afflicted and put in bondage by the devil.
- (viii) Christians who are also covenant children of God, who are in various kinds of spiritual or physical bondage deserved to be loosed (Delivered, set free).
- (ix) It was a ruler of the synagogue "Parish Pastor" that opposed Jesus Christ's deliverance ministry, that the Sabbath was more important. Those who are contending against deliverance ministry for Christians today are also Church theologians and leaders
- (x) Most Church leaders like the ruler of the synagogue (Contemporary Church) are not compassionate about the physical and spiritual bondage their members are in, nor are they keen about their deliverance.
- (xi) Jesus Christ is a compassionate and good shepherd who seek the total deliverance and prosperity of His followers. He gave priority to this than any other religious commitment.

Many Christians like this "DAUGHTER OF ABRAHAM" are being oppressed by various kinds of devils resulting into physical and spiritual bondage. Whether infirmity, poverty, wretchedness, emotional disorder, barrenness, sexual immorality, mental disorder, infertility, unsuccessfulness, indebtedness, marital failure; so many to name. They deserve to be "loosed" from those bondages. The works of

Satan must be destroyed in their lives. Loosing is one of the major divine authority the Lord has given us to destroy all the "wicked tares" of the enemy operating against God's will in the lives of Christians.

Many are just dormant allowing the devil to continue hurting them in various aspects of their life. Jesus has commissioned you into the ministry of binding and loosing. Stand up now! Bind and loose. If you don't bind those things you are suppose to bind, they will eventually put you in bondage. If you don't loose the things you are suppose to loose, those things will put you in bondage.

COME ON BIND AND LOOSE NOW!

So many Christians today have been bound in the area of their health, finances, marriage, childbearing, emotions, family relationship, the enterprises of their hands, and other endeavors of life. They are stocked either in the parlance of ignorance or spiritual passiveness.

One of the common manifestations of demonic control or being in bondage is the passivity that is induced. The person who is being oppressed at will is inert, his mind is dull and his spirit is torpid and lifeless. He resigns to a state of not reasoning on what next action to take. The danger of passivity is that it gives Satan all the initiatives and this will make the passive Christian loose the battle by default.

Most times Christians love to be in a defensive position. They only allow the devil to strike first before they react. Fighting only when you are attacked by the devil is very inadequate, at best it only prevents defeat, it never wins a war.

The Biblical principle demands on us to always attack, which is why the Bible gives no instructions for defensive positions. The Lord always urges His people to go ahead, take the battle to the enemies' gates to possess them. Joshua was ordered to go out and fight the Amalekites, David, the shepherd boy ran out to fight Goliath. Our Lord and master Jesus was led by the Spirit of God into the wilderness to encounter Satan. Attacks seize the initiative from the enemy; dictates the terms of the battle and chooses the ground on which it will be fought. You have no excuse to remain in bondage, loose youself now in Jesus name.

CHAPTER EIGHT

BELIEVERS VICTORY OVER SATAN

The Lion of Judah, king of Kings, our Lord Jesus Christ has given us perfect victory over the devil and his demons. Our responsibility is to enforce and keep the victory and live our lives as victorious Christians. Our victory over demonic power is clearly stated in:

> *"And having disarmed and defeated principalities and power, ruling demonic spirits. He made a public show of them, triumphing over them" (Amplified).*
> <u>Colossians 2:15</u>

Every Christian has been bequeathed this victory of Christ's triumph over satan with His blood on the Cross of Calvary. He has the authority and legal right to command the devil and his demons where to go and what to do. In <u>James 4:7</u> God gave us this personal guarantee: *"Submit yourselves therefore to God, resist the devil, and he will flee"* The word "submit" means to come under authority. Christians are implored implicitly to be totally obedient to the Lord. When we submit in obedience to the Lord, His authority comes upon us. It is under this authority that we can boldly stand up with our armour to firmly resist the devil and his demons.

Let us recall the story in **Luke 10:17-20**

> *"And the seventy returned again with joy, saying Lord even the devils are subject unto us through thy name. And he said unto them, I beheld Satan as lightning fall from heaven.*
>
> *Behold, I Give unto you power to tread on serpents and scorpions, and over all the power of the enemy: and nothing shall by any means hurt you:*
>
> *"<u>Not withstanding in this rejoice not that the spirits are subject unto you; but rather rejoice, because your names are written in heaven.</u>"*

Though the disciples were excited about their triumph over the devils but the Lord responded to their report with these unusual words in verse 20:

> *"Notwithstanding in this rejoice not, that spirits are subject unto you; but rather rejoice, because your names are written in heaven".*

Here Jesus made them understand that the source of their authority was not merely their commanding those demons to obey them in His name but their relationship with Him as their Lord. It takes more than the right words to face and confront devil; IT TAKES THE RIGHT RELATIONSHIP WITH GOD. When we walk in faith and in obedience, we have the inexhaustible authority and power to resisit the devil and make him flee.

We are in the age of increasing demonic activites as predicted in **_1 Tim. 4:1;2 Tim. 3:1._** Our age is characterised by an ever - increasing flood of satanic wickedness ranging from psychic afflictions to moral aberrations. In as much as these forces against which the believer and the church must contend are spiritual, they can only be effectively withstood and overcome by spiritual armour and spiritual weapons.

For without faith and the empowering of the Holy Spirit, the church is practically helpless and defeated. We are authorised by virtue of our heavenly position to put up a bold resistance in the name and authority of Jesus Christ against satan and he must obey! **_(Mark 16:17;Luke 9:1)_**

Boldly confess the efficacious power of the blood of Jesus, for the strength of our authority rests in this alone **_Rev. 12:11_** **_"For they overcame him (Satan) by the blood of the Lamb, and by the word of their testimony"._** Satan always gives way before the faith of a Christian who courageously pleads the power of Jesus' blood. His temptations, oppressions and works can be effectively defeated by the appeal to the blood of Jesus Christ. During deliverance ministry we have heard demons screaming out loud at the mention of the blood of Jesus because it torments them terribly.

In **_Ephesians 6:16_** believers are expected by the shield of faith to quench all of satan's darts.

"Above all taking the shield of faith, wherewith ye shall be able to quench all the fiery darts of the wicked". We do this as we exercise our faith in Jesus Christ. God never provides partial protection for His own; when we trust Him to do what He has said He will do, we have complete protection . If we are relying on Christ, satan's fire tipped arrows will be put out before they can do their damage. But if we do not rely on Christ to be our strength when temptations come, we will be vulnerable to his attacks and will experience serious frustration in our Christian life.

PRAYER THE BATTLE AXE

In order for the believers to stand victorious in the conflict even with their complete armours, there must be constant and earnest prayer. It is through prayer of faith that the believers' armour is first put on, and then becomes effective. Since prayer is associated here with warfare, the indication is that prayer itself is part of the battle. In fact, prayer is conflict in itself, and it is vital in the spiritual warfare in which every believer is involved, because it is the central function of the new life of faith, the very heartbeat of our life in God.

Believers are implored in **_Ephesian 6:18_** that praying and watching should be done with all perseverance. This does not mean that we defeat the devil by working and striving in prayer, for we have already seen that he is already defeated because of Christ's work on the cross. We are only fighting a good fight by means of prayer, executing our redemptive authority offensively against the devil.

Prayer is effectual when it has its origin with God. Almighty God sees the whole battle field and knows the devil's plans. He directs the movements of the entire spiritual army. He is the Lord of Hosts.

He also implants in us our prayer for spiritual victory. God communicates to us through the Holy spirit the prayer we are to pray. The Holy Spirit lays the proper burden on us and He motivates and gives us the thoughts to pray. **_Romans 8:26_** says *"Likewise the Spirit also helpeth our infirmities: for we know not what we should pray for as we ought: but the Spirit itself maketh intercession for us with groanings which cannot be uttered"* So it is God who gives the deep sense of urgency for prayer and also gives assurance of victory.

Since God has assured us of answers to our prayers and the Bible says the fervent and effectual prayer of the righteous availeth much, therefore we ought to prevail in our prayer. There is the urgent need for us to travail in prayers because the devil has gone rampaging, because he knows his time is very short. In many instances the history of the church shows that the greatest men who have lived to shake the world for Christ with God's power have been, every one of them, men of prevailing prayer.

The devil in all his wisdom knows that the power of prayer is the greatest weapon that God has put in our hands against him. He understands better than we do, what prayer means to us and to others. He knows that it is only Holy Spirit baptized Christians that were empowered to frustrate and mess him up. **_Luke 10:19_** explains. That is why his chief attack is directed against our prayer life.

> *The devil in all his wisdom knows that the power of prayer is the greatest weapon that God has put in our hands against him. He understands better than we do, what prayer means to us and to others. He knows that it is only Holy Spirit baptized Christians that were empowered to frustrate and mess him up.*

Satan and his agents fear the believer who knows how to prevail with God in prayer. They don't like a bit Christians who are **"Strong in the Lord and in the power of His might"**. **_(Ephesians 6:10:)_** and who are prayer warriors. They are very comfortable with lazy, prayerless, lukewarm and backsliding Christians who are often weak in their prayer life. These are the kind of Christians who see prayer as a burden. I normally call this specie the **"ICE CREAM CHRISTIANS"** who once a while pray **"ICE CREAM"** prayers. May God help them. (Amen).

Those who are not Holy Spirit baptized Christians are their slaves, they deal with them the way they like. If you are not a true believer of Jesus Christ you are in their net. The church of Jesus Christ is the only body in the world given power and authority to resist the devil and destroy his evil machinations and this omnipotent power of the Almighty God works in and through Spirit filled Christians by the Holy Spirit.

> ***Thou art my battle axe and weapons of war for with thee will (the Lord) break in pieces the nations, and with thee will I destroy kingdoms"***
> ***(Jeremiah 51:20:)***
>
> ***"Verily I say unto you, whatsoever ye shall bind on earth shall be bound in heaven (Spirit realm): and whatsoever ye shall loose on earth be loosed in heaven (Spirit realm)" (Amplified)***
> ***(Mathew 18:18)***

For this reason, Satan mobilizes every thing he can command in order to prevent a believer from praying. He has a ready made device which is planted in the old Adamic nature of the flesh; the uncrucifed human nature (flesh) that is always in constant conflict with the Spirit. He will normally attack a believer through the lust of the flesh which gives him access to the believer's soul.

If you start to pray through, you are going to meet with real battle in the spirit realm. Often times many believers have come to me complaining: that the more they get involved in serious spiritual warfare prayers the more wicked and spontaneous attacks they received from the devil. I have always told them that is a good result. It means their prayers are hitting the devil very hard, therefore they should continue in their prayers. Those counter attacks from the devil is to put fear in them so that they can stop praying further.

This is a real spiritual conflict. It is a struggle between the spirit of man and that of the enemy, an engagement of spirit with spirit and the Holy Spirit is standing by the side of God's people. And the Bible says:

> *"But the salvation of the righteous is of the Lord: he is their strength in the time of trouble. And the Lord shall help them, and deliver them: he shall deliver them from the wicked, and save them, because they trust in Him".*
> *(Psalm 37:39-40)*

The following are the commonly used devices by the devil to take away our desire to pray:

(i) Tiredness (viii) procrastination
(ii) Over eating (ix) Discouragement
(iii) Excessive sleeping (x) Depression
(v) Over busyness (xi) Problems
(vi) Recurring guiltiness (xii) Eating, Drinking and
(vii) Doubthaving sexual intercoursein the dream.

Prayers made in Jesus name to Almighty God is the link between the natural and the supernatural, the possible and the impossible. Powers of darkness are paralysed by effective prayers. No wonder satan tries to keep our minds fussy in active work until we cannot have time to pray.

Our so called work for God without prayer is nonsense. The truth is that we do not work for God. We are to be loyal to Him, so that by His sovereign will He can work through us. God reckons on us for extreme service. To be very busy in worldly pursuits in order to satisfy the cravings of our insatiable desires without prayer is dangerous and disastrous. When these pursuits have become the centre point of our private life, we need urgent fellowship with the Holy Spirit, otherwise we could be plotting the early destruction of our soul.

Prayer will give the full estimate of the place of the Holy Spirit in a Christian's life. But we must resist the ploys of the devil by praying always. The believer who fails to pray is praying to fail.

The Holy Spirit, when invited, would first of all destroy your private life and later reorganize it into a thoroughfare for God to work in and through you His will and purposes. Prayer will give the full estimate of the place of the Holy Spirit in a Christian's life. But we must resist the ploys of the devil by praying always. The believer who fails to pray is praying to fail.

DISCERNING AN EFFECTIVE ARMOUR

Every person who experiences new birth in Christ undergoes regeneration, and a continuing recreation of the image of Christ within his personality. This new life is transmitted to the soul by the indwelling spirit *(Titus 3:4-5).* The Holy Spirit mediates the full grace of the Godhead to the believer and helps him or her to operate with specific gifts.

Discernment is one of such gifts the Holy spirit bestows upon some Christians. It is one of the most effective reconnaissance weapon in spiritual warfare. If you are a true child of God, the battle line is drawn between you and the devil.

The gift of discernment is a divine assistance you can receive for your spiritual warfare.

Discernment is the ability given by the Holy Spirit to a Christian to distinguish good from evil, truth from error. The purpose of discernment is to see what God has for us to enable us walk rightly in His ways. This ability will caution believers from falling away from the faith, keep them on guard against the wiles of their adversary the devil. The writer of Hebrews spoke of discernment as an element of maturity.

> *"But strong meat belongeth to them that are full of age, even those who by reason of use have their senses exercised to discern both good and evil"* **Heb 5:14.**

Discernment in the general sense, is God's given armour for believers to guide them in the path of truth and to enable them investigate subtle snares and devices of the devil especially familiar spirits who are closely lurking around.

DISCERNING OF SPIRIT

Beyond the position of discernments for all believers by the Holy Spirit is *"the ability to distinguish between spirits"*. **(1 Corinthians 12: 10).** Discerning of spirit is the gift the Holy Spirit bestows on believers to enable them accurately detect and distinguish the identities of spirits and their activities.

The real explanation of this gift of the discerning of spirit is that God wants those who have this gift to have revelations of the plans and purposes of the enemy and their forces; also to enable them identify spirits. We have two types of world. We have that of human beings which is visible and can be discerned with our five senses of: sight, hearing, taste, smell and touch and that of the spirits which is invisible and cannot be discerned with our five physical senses. We all believe that there is God, yet we have not seen Him before. This is because God is a Spirit.

Discerning of spirit also consists of spiritual discrimination endowed by the Holy Spirit for the purpose of judging the source of power whether human, satanic or of God. When your spiritual eyes are opened by the Holy Spirit you will be able to see evil spirits and angels.

The gift of seeing spiritual things will make the job of a minister of God to become easy. In *(Judges 6:11-16):* Gideons's spiritual eyes were opened and he saw an angel that told him God's purpose for his life. In *(Luke 1:26-28.)* the angel of God came to tell Mary that she will conceive and have a baby whose name would be called Jesus the Son of God, even though she was a virgin. She saw an angel.

> *If you cannot discern the appropriate demon responsible for an evil act, you will definitely be binding and casting the wrong evil spirit. Discerning of spirit is very important to "Prayer warrior" Christians, ministers of God especially those in the deliverance ministry.*

Discerning of spirit is a very strategic weapon for spiritual warfare. It is a "secret service" weapon used to identify various kinds of demon; their locations and mode of operations.

A believer will be able to spy on the activities of the devil with this Holy Spirit gift and let him know what appropriate offensive tactic he needs to take. Unless you locate your problems you might not be able to dislocate them. If you cannot discern the appropriate demon responsible for an evil act, you will definitely be binding and casting the wrong evil spirit. Discerning of spirit is very important to "Prayer warrior" Christians, ministers of God especially those in the deliverance ministry.

One Friday night as I was preparing to go and have a rest before our vigil prayer travail, a pastor friend and his wife came to visit me and opted to join in this all night prayer.

I left them in my office and went upstairs to my bedroom. Immediately I got to my bedroom the Holy Spirit ordered me to return to my office and begin deliverance ministry for the Pastor's wife before it will be 12:00 midnight. I initialy hesitated because it will be embarrassing to the Pastor and his wife. I had no option but to obey the Holy Spirit. When I got to my office the Pastor's wife was already manifesting in a very subtle manner. She was complaining that my office was too hot and the windows should be opened. The husband and other people who were with her in my office were surprised because the air-conditioner was functioning perfectly well and the room was very cold and chilly.

The truth was that she was actually being tormented by the presence of the Blood of Jesus Christ covering my office and the Holy Spirit. She was possessed by the Queen of the coast (marine spirit) and other evil spirits; they could not withstand the Blood of Jesus Christ that was tormenting them, so they began to manifest through her. Yet her Pastor husband could not discern this manifestation.

Immediately, I held her up to the surprise of the husband and another minister of God and commenced a deliverance ministry. This Pastor's wife manifested so violently to the shock and amazement of her husband. During the first session of deliverance ministry that ended 11:50 pm she vehemently refused to confess that Jesus Christ is come in the flesh and He is the Son of God. The husband who was witnessing the ministration almost collapsed, he could not believe with his eyes. But thank God that she was finally delivered.

Imagine a Pastor married to a mammy water (Queen of the sea) spirit possessed wife; they live together, pray together, go to church together but he could not discern the spirit possessing his wife after five years of marriage. I have also ministered to several ministers of God who have suffered this kind of fate, they normally have problems with their churches and ministries. They can never succeed. No minister of God can succeed in his calling with a demon possessed wife, because the two are one.

It is good to discern spirits. **NOT EVERYONE THAT IS CALLING JESUS IS ACTUALLY BORN AGAIN!** There are so many of satan agents in the church assigned to perpetuate evil. They are often very active and dedicated in church activites. Becareful of the so called Christian sister or brother you want to marry, she or he might not be the kind of believer you think. She or he could be possessed of evil spirits. Prayerfully ask the Holy Spirit for proper guidance. May God help us. (Amen)

Each of these two gifts of discernment and discerning of spirit must be tested, at times the prompting from God may be mixed with the motivations of the man involved in its delivery. In order for these gifts to function properly, there must be accountability, the testing of their faithfulness.

Although, all Christians can cultivate spiritual discernment gift, some are given discernment as a specific gift of the Holy Spirit. The discerners of spirit must humbly depend on God, they need to learn how to wait on the Lord and watch for His signals. True discerners always operate with God's own love, mercy and patience, as well as with His power.

In our life journeys as believers on this earth, the Lord Himself is our preserver, He has promised He will never leave us alone. He will be with us unto the end of the world

> ***1 John 5:1** says: "We know that whosoever is born of God sinneth not: but Jesus Christ will keep him safe and the evil one does not touch him" (Amplified).*

It is also our responsibility as Christians to stay away from sin. **SHUN EVIL!** We must quickly acknowledge our sins when committed, repent of them, appropriate the faithfulness of God to forgive us our trespasses.

One cool evening sometimes in June, 1997 a tall and lanky man sauntered into our secretariat, he was looking physically drained and fatigued. He had just terminated a five hour journey by road from Warri where he was directed to come and see me for counselling and possibly ministration.

As he was ushered into my office I could discern frustration, hopelessness and the handwritings of demons all over his body. After a brief prayer, I asked him what the matter was, his reply became a long excursion into his life history. And this was his story:

> *"I am a Born Again Christian, an Elder in my Church. I'm no more a young man; Evangelist you can see for yourself I am in my fifties; I'm not married. All my businesses have collapsed; hindrance all over*

the places. I have sold my cars and most of my other properties to enable me survive. Nothing I ever laid hands on have prospered".

I have prayed, believed, fasted, and gone through several counselling sessions and series of deliverance ministratons; I have tarried many nights; several ministers of God have prayed with me and even anointed me. All these to no avail. Nothing has changed for good. I was directed by a minister of God in Warri to come and see you."

While he was talking to me I keyed my spirit into the Holy Spirit for unction and wisdom. Quickly, the Holy Spirit told me to ask this brother what happened to him twenty three years ago and where did he go to seek spiritual help and succour. After a while, he was able to establish that twenty three years ago was 1974. That is the Holy Spirit for you, taking us twenty three years back in restropection.

He also recollected to have gone with some friends that same 1974 to consult a Witch Doctor for divine protection, charms for prosperity and security. After soliciting for the services of this agent of satan every affairs of his life turned upside down. This was the beginning of his sorrows. It was woes upon woes in a daily, monthly and yearly basis. Things were never the same again. This Christian brother ignorantly, when he has yet to give his life to Jesus Christ, entered into unholy accords with the devil.

His calamities have remained because up till when he came to me he has not been able to locate the root cause of his problems inspite of his marathon prayers, fasting and spiritual warfares. The first solution was for him to identify the cause before going into unneccessary confessions of scriptures and spiritual warfares.

Many believers are suffering this kind of experience because of their ignorance. A lack of knowledge leads to blindness and gross spiritual darkness. Don't forget that it is satan and familiar spirits that rule the realm of darkness. Those who walk in darkness will always fall victims of the powers of darkness. God warned His people against the danger of ignorance in *Isaiah 5:13a* *"Therefore my people are gone into captivity, because they have no knowkledge'*

His calamities have remained because up till when he came to me he has not been able locate the root cause of his problems inspite of his marathon prayers, fasting and spiritual warfares. The first solution was for him to identify the cause before going into unneccessary confessions of scriptures and spiritual warfares.

Knowledge destroys ignorance. Knowledge is strength, it brings deliverance. Knowledge is light.

> *".... but through knowledge shall the just be delivered".*
> *Proverb 11:19.*

Knowledge is also a key to abundant riches and strength. *"And by knowledge shall the chambers be filled with all precious and pleasant riches. A wise man is strong; yea, a man of knowledge increaseth strength."*
(Proverb 24:4-5)

It is loud foolishness for any Christian to presume that because he or she is now in Christ, familiar spirits will not execute the previous agreements they have with him or her, if he or she has not renounced and annulled such accords with the authority of Jesus Christ.

To cut the story short, I told our brother from Warri that the root cause of his problems was the previous deals he struck with that Witch Doctor twenty three years ago; and because he did not appropriate his legal authority in Jesus Christ to specifically renounce and revoke them, those destructive demons became his unseen enemies.

It is loud foolishness for any Christian to presume that because he or she is now in Christ, familiar spirits will not execute the previous agreements they have with him

After counselling and ministering, our brother is now a happy person. Praise God! This is the **LAW OF HARVEST,** it is a universal spiritual law governing every human being whether you are a believer in Christ or not; whatever a man sows he will surely reap:

> *"Be not deceived; God is not mocked: for whatsoever a man soweth, that shall he also reap for he that soweth to his flesh shall of the flesh reap corruption; but he that soweth to the Spirit shall of the Spirit reap life everlasting."*
> *(Galatians 6:7-8)*

Our redemptive positon is to enable us turn to Christ to deal with controlling spirits, so that curses and covenants can be broken and not a guarantee for us to continue in sin. It is very important to note that only believers in Jesus Christ have the legal right and inherent authority to revoke and annul curses and covenants incurred in their lives because of the redemptive work Christ has done for them on the Cross of Calvary.

We must also understand that we have to live with the consequences of our decisions in this fallen life, even though we are forgiven through our faith in Christ Jesus. Our duty is to appropriate what Jesus Christ has done on the cross when we turn to Him in righteousness. If you don't repent from your sin, you will break the hedge and assuredly the serpent (devil)will bite you - ***Eccl. 10:8 God forbid!***

Are you a believer of Jesus Christ? Do you have the Holy Spirit indwell in you? If you are not and have decided to put your faith in Jesus say this prayer:

> **Lord Jesus Christ, I believe in my heart that you are the son of God who came from heaven to die on the cross and through the death of your body I receive forgiveness of sin from Almighty God. I thank you for redeeming my soul from eternal destruction by your blood. Right now, Lord Jesus Christ, I welcome you into my heart as my Lord and Saviour; send me the Holy Spirit to come and dwell in me forever. Amen!**

TESTIMONIES

"And when He called His twelve disciples to Him, He gave them power over unclean spirits (Demons), TO CAST THEM OUT, and TO HEAL all kinds of sickness and all kinds of disease."
(Matthew 10:1)

These testimonies are few among the great numbers of miracles, signs and wonders the Holy Spirit has done through Jesus Christ Power World Evangelism and the servant of God Evangelist John Deby Edukugho. They were experienced after deliverance ministrations and during seminars, revival and crusade meetings.

HEALED OF 11 YEARS DIABETIES

I suffered from diabetes for 11 years and this affliction caused me to use three insulin injections daily. I basically expended all money to seek medical cure to no avail. My wife was introduced to the Evangelist and she brought me to him. And when I met him he asked "Do you BELIEVE JESUS CAN HEAL YOU?" I said yes I believe. He then said. Stop taking your insulin injection, tomorrow come fasting for Deliverance Ministration. I initially hesitated because I know what I suffer whenever I am off insulin injection. The Evangelist prayed for me and insisted I stop the insulin injection medication, I obeyed.

By the third day of my deliverance he ordered me to throw away all my medication into the bin. I obeyed, after my deliverance ministration I was totally healed. God is the great healer. To Him be the glory forever.

OBOH B.O.

EVANGELIST'S COMMENT:

This Brother was actually afflicted with Diabetes by their housemaid who was possessed of witchcraft spirit. I discerned this during counselling session. Two weeks after brother Oboh's deliverance ministration, the housemaid publicly confessed to be possessed of witchraft spirit and have been responsible for his affliction. May God deliver you from the hands of your enemies? Amen.

EMPLOYED AFTER 13 YEARS OF JOBLESSNESS

I am a University graduate for thirteen years seeking for employment in various private and public companies, military and security agencies to no avail. The results are always the same "SORRY WE CAN'T HELP YOU". This evil circle persisted for thirteen years in spite of marathon prayers I have engaged in. I sought counselling and spiritual assistance with various ministers of God all to no avail. I became frustrated. One fateful day, one of my aunties visited me in my junior sister's house where I live and heard of my situation, she quickly insisted I should go to JESUS CHRIST POWER WORLD EVANGELISM to see the servant of God - Evangelist John Deby Edukugho. I summoned courage to go, because I was wearied of consulting men of God. I met him, after counselling me, he made a prophetic statement to me "THE SIEGE IS OVER" "YOU HAVE COME TO YOUR LAST BUS STOP OF THE EVIL JOURNEY OF YOUR LIFE" I said Amen.

During the deliverance ministration I remembered he prayed thus "HOLY SPIRIT GIVE ME A SWORD TO CUT OFF TODAY EVERY SATANIC CHAIN USED TO TIE YOUR SON (ERNEST) FROM THE ALTAR OF THE WICKED DEVILS!. And I saw him cut off invisible chain from my legs and hands. Two weeks after my deliverance ministrations I got a job with a top class company, with fat salary and a car given to me. Praised the Lord!

ERNEST (Lagos)

EVANGELIST'S COMMENTS:

In <u>Matthew 18:18</u> Jesus gave us the authority to BIND AND LOOSE. There are things to BIND and things to LOOSE. The Lord opened my eyes to see that Brother

Ernest was bound with **EVIL CHAINS**. Many Christians have been bound in many areas of their lives by wicked devils and they are ignorant of this and they remain bound. Jesus said until we loose some things, heaven will not loose, until we bind some things, heaven will not bind. But the truth is that you can only **LOOSE** and **BIND** what you have knowledge of. Therefore the problem of Christians remain. *"MY PEOPLE ARE DESTROYED BECAUSE THEY LACK SPIRITUAL KNOWLEDGE" (Hosea 4:6)*

HEALED OF 9 YEARS ISSUE OF BLOOD

I have been afflicted by persistent flow of blood for 9 years. I changed two menstrual pads every day. I have consulted both Orthodox and Modern medical experts and applied all the medication they offered to no avail. I heard about EVANGELIST JOHN DEBY EDUKUGHO coming to hold a four days crusade in our country Cameroon, precisely Douala Stadium. I made up my mind to attend. During the second night of the crusade after preaching he asked all those who needed healing of any kind of diseases and sickness to come out. I quickly ran out. And he said "ALL THE HOLY SPIRIT WANTS YOU PEOPLE TO DO IS TO DANCE WITH JOY AND PRAISES TO HIM, AND AS YOU ARE DANCING, PRAISING THE LORD, YOUR HEALING IS TAKING PLACE" I was surprised because I have not seen this dancing method of healing before, but I made up my mind to believe the servant of God. As the choir rendered the songs I danced with great joy and praises to the Lord. When I got home I noticed I was dry, and that was the end of my 9 years persistent blood flow. What an awesome God we serve!

MERCY *(Cameroon)*

EVANGELIST'S COMMENT:

Obedience was the key to this sister's healing. God can heal us in various kinds of ways, all we need do is to HAVE FAITH IN GOD AND BELIEVE IN HIS PROPHETS (2Chronicles 20:20). Many have lost their opportunities for healing because they are accustomed to one pattern of healng. Our God is mighty. He has millions of ways to achieve one single purpose.

DELIVERED FROM 12 YEARS BARRENESS

I am a believer in the Lord, married but suffered 12 years of barreness. Every medical investigations and reports showed that both my husband and I were medically okay to have children. I have offered all manners of prayers and fasting without any fruitful result. One day a brother in - law recommended JESUS CHRIST POWER WORLD EVANGELISM to us. He claimed that God is doing great and marvelous miracles of Salvation, Signs and Wonders in the ministry, especially through His servant Evangelist John Deby Edukugho.

I met with him, during counselling session he made a prophetic statement "I DON'T CARE HOW LONG YOU HAVE BEEN IN THIS CONDITION AS FAR AS YOU ARE NOT OLDER THAN SARAH - ABRAHAM'S WIFE YOU WILL SURELY CONCEIVE AND HAVE YOUR CHILDREN." He spoke with every divine boldness and conviction. After continuous prayers, I conceived and give birth to a baby Girl. Praise the lord!
GRACE CHUKWUDI

EVANGELIST'S COMMENT:
Prayer works! keep praying, prayer do affect heaven. Your miracle is on the way. It is never too late with God.

The answer to your prayer is for an appointed time; nevertheless, some anointing can provoke quick answers to prayers. All the same keep praying!

MOTHER AND CHILDREN HEALED OF 3 YEARS LEPROSY

My two daughters and I were afflicted with leprosy through satanic bewitchment. A neighbour invited us to Evangelist John Deby Edukugho's crusade at Ife stadium. We were half way into the crusade, when thunderstorm began to blast, suddenly the whole cloud became dark this was about 6:45pm. The heaven opened with a heavy downpour of rain. Because the stadium was uncovered, people began to run out, to them this concluded the meeting. In spite of this heavy downpour the Evangelist continued preaching inside the rain. All his clothes were drenched with water. Many were surprise at him. Some ministers of God were suggesting closing the meeting. Nevertheless a small size of the number of the attendants remained, encouraged by the Evangelist tenacity. My daughters and I decided to remain. At the end of the preaching the Evangelist prophesied. "FOR WAITING IN THIS RAIN, ALL YOUR DISEASES ARE WASHED AWAY, COME TOMORROW AND TESTIFY". By next morning when my daughters and I woke up, we noticed that all the leprosy in our hands have disappeared. Our skin were like that of a new born baby. We ran to the stadium the next evening to share our testimonies. More testimonies of great miracles and healing were experienced by those of us who waited in the rain. Praise the Lord!
   BIMBO S. (IFE)

EVANGELIST'S COMMENTS:

Many Christians are used to serving God only when they are comfortable. Blessed are those who sow (wait) in tears (drenched in the rain) they will reap (healed) in joy. Be ready to serve your God come rain come shine!

TO ORDER TAPES OF JOHN DEBY EDUKUGHO, COUNSELLLING, AND SPEAKING ENGAGEMENT.

CONTACT:

**JOHN DEBY EDUKUGHO
JESUS CHRIST POWER WORLD EVANGELISM
38 CAMDIKE STREET
VALLEY STREAM, NEW YORK, 11580.
Website: www.jcpwe.org
E-mail:debyjcp@yahoo.com**